O SHINING LIGHT

cum autem venerit quod perfectum est
evacuabitur quod ex parte est

but when the perfect comes,
the partial will pass away

I Corinthians 13:10

O Shining Light

Old English Meditations
for Advent and Christmastide

Introduction and Commentary by
Jacob and Mamie Riyeff

Translated by
Jacob Riyeff

Illustrations by
Daniel Mitsui

GRACEWING

Typeset by Word and Page, Chester, UK

Cover design by Bernardita Peña Hurtado

CONTENTS

FOREWORD

Sometimes the best way to renew the present is to delve into the past—delve deeply, let's say, a thousand years. If your liturgical interest in vernacular English is flagging, this treasure trove buried in the ancient Exeter Book is sure to dazzle. Lifted from the oldest anthology of English lyrics, this masterful rendition of *The Advent Lyrics* updates and preserves the charm and freshness of the original Old English. Here is liturgical vernacular of the first waters!

In the final days of Advent, from 17 to 24 December, a haunting series of antiphons are sung, each beginning with an expressive invocation of longing—O! This is followed by some title of Christ. Each day brings some new title, some facet of the one we are awaiting. Monks give these antiphons honored position at Vespers for the Song of Mary, and in parish liturgy they precede the Gospel. These O Antiphons count down the last days of Advent and build up an ever-richer understanding of the mystery to come.

With use over the years they have become ever more beloved to me, and my mind hungers for a fuller expansion on the content. That is precisely what is offered by the early Anglo-Saxon monks in this poem from their tenth-century collection. Here blows a fresh wind from a time when faith was simpler, more direct and immediate. This rendition retains both the timbre and the poetic technique, with use of alliteration on initial syllables, two per verse.

Several Advent O antiphons, other than the ones we are familiar with, are included here. Each is given a lyrical expansion rich in metaphor and narrative flair. These help us to step into the sacred story and afford us additional purchase on the mystery being contemplated. Jacob and Mamie Riyeff take us a step further in a commentary section which outlines the progress of thought and theme in each lyric. These are somewhat in the nature of verbal "illumi-nations" and highlight the complex and divergent track of thought in the lyrics.

For those who are seeking Advent reading, this volume provides reflections from another era and, more than that, a joining in faith and communion with people from a mil-lennium ago.

Br. Paul Quenon, OCSO
Abbey of Our Lady of Gethsemani

Acknowledgements

We are grateful for the many people who have helped us get this book together. Special thanks go to Br. Paul Quenon, OCSO, for providing a beautiful foreword and a living link to the Western monastic tradition from which this poem springs forth; Daniel Mitsui for providing compelling and lovely visual accents appropriate to the poetry; Jacob's former student Joseph Sizemore for getting the Old English text together for us; Columbia University Press for permitting us to reprint the Old English text; and Tom Longford and Clive Tolley at Gracewing who made this book with all its bells and whistles come to fruition.

Mamie. My first thanks go to my children Clara, Selevan, and Abram: your very existence has led me to thirst for Jesus in ways I never understood possible before you were a part of your father's and my lives. My sincere thanks go to the women who so warmly welcomed me to Milwaukee and have walked with me on this journey: Sara Larson, Anh Clausen, Rachel McGrew, Darcy Lesniak, and all of the ladies in Beacon Moms. I am grateful to my family of origin—Joe and Kathy Scott, Bridget, Bethany, and Alex— for your love, support, and encouragement throughout the years to always find my purpose and live a life filled with abundance. And finally, I thank Jacob for inviting me to collaborate with him on this writing project: his desire and passion to send *The Advent Lyrics* out into the world was my inspiration to continue the work after full days of parenting three young children. *Deo Gratias!*

Jacob. My first thanks go to all those who read *The Advent Lyrics* aloud with me every December during my time at the University of Notre Dame. Each winter break we'd gather in O'Shaughnessy's Great Hall and read the poem in Old English in its entirety, whether we knew what we were saying or not: Andrew Klein, Amanda Shaw (now Sr. Diana Marie of Christ Jesus, OP), Jessica Hughes, Megan Hall, Melissa Mayus, Emily Ransom, Tom Hall, and Erica Machulak all read one year or another. Thanks also to all the Bacon Dads (a joke name based on Mamie's serious group named above) who read Old English poems in translation with me in 2018, and to David Craig for his encouragement with Old English translation and three of these lyrics' first appearance in my chapbook he published in 2015. My deepest appreciation as ever to Sr. Pascaline Coff, OSB, for bringing me into the Benedictine world, and to my wife Mamie for her love and support and, now, for her collaborative work with me on this volume.

Milwaukee, Wisconsin
Feast of St. Boniface

INTRODUCTION

Why did we write this devotional book for Advent and Christmas based on a thousand-year-old poem? Strangely enough, because we have three small children. It's a round-about reason, but the process started there. When our older two children reached the age when they could actively participate in devotions and know that feast days were something special, we realized that the attention we paid to the liturgical seasons through daily Scripture reading, Mass, the celebration of the Liturgy of the Hours, and informative reading online, while good as modeling for the children, would not help them in the same way these practices helped us. So, as parents do, we started thinking of ways to help them understand the liturgical seasons that were more attuned to their lives and understanding: finally getting an Advent wreath for the house, constructing a Jesse Tree with paper cutouts and Scripture passages, attending the "King cake" party on Epiphany at our parish, indulging in sweets and media conspicuously less during Lent, etc.

The present book is of course not a children's book at all. But realizing that our children needed to be informed about the liturgical seasons in ways appropriate to them in order to be formed by them was a mental and spiritual adjustment for both of us. In addition, over the last few years, we've also both become involved in moms' and dads' groups in our large parish family here in the Archdiocese of Milwaukee. Leading these groups has gotten us both thinking about how to draw out the meaning and lessons of each liturgical season for the spiritual lives of adults with widely varying degrees of cultural, theological, and historical commitments and backgrounds.

One of us (Jacob) studies medieval poetry, and a couple of years ago some of the men in his group asked him to share one of the earliest English poems during Lent. Much to his surprise, it went so well that they asked him to do another. This follow-up session went so well too that Jacob thought that other Christians eager to find out about the many treasures of the Church's long tradition might find interest in these old poetic relics as well. One of us (Mamie) does not study medieval poetry, so she has a good eye for how *not* to talk about medieval poetry among people who have not encountered it before. Together, we thought one early English poem that would be especially accessible and edifying for a broader modern audience was *The Advent Lyrics*, a poem that treats profoundly and beautifully the symbols and spirit of Advent and Christmastide.

In a poem like this, modern Christians can find a link to the deep past of the Church. The English language has some of the oldest recorded poetry in the West, much of it relating directly to the lived expression of and meditation on the life of faith. As Brother Paul Quenon suggests in his foreword, we think that turning to these ancient works from our tradition can be refreshing and enlightening. Old works such as *The Advent Lyrics* have different ways of thinking, knowing, and representing than most of us are used to, but they are still part of a shared culture among a community that has persisted throughout the centuries. They still wrestle with the same mysteries of the faith and of being human. With this commonality and clear difference, poems like *The Advent Lyrics* can help us experience the faith anew through what the modern British poet Geoffrey Hill called a "strange likeness".

In part to highlight this "strange likeness" (the continuity and distance we have with our own past), this book includes both a modern English translation and the original Old English text on facing pages. As you read the translation, we invite you to turn your gaze to the thousand-year old words across the page and think about the monk or clerk who wrote them down on parchment somewhere in

England so long ago, even if you are not familiar with Old English at all. This ancient language is the ancestor of the language spoken by all English speakers today, regardless of their ethnic or geographical origins. While Old English came from a particular place and time, it also belongs to anyone who speaks or writes in English today. The sights and sounds of Old English can be fun and enriching even without any training—no need to be intimidated. The sights are here, but if you would like to hear the Old English being read aloud, you can visit jacobriyeff.com for audio files of Jacob reading *The Advent Lyrics* in the original. However you choose to interact with everything we have gathered here, we invite you to experience the "strange likeness" of this translation of *The Advent Lyrics* as you encounter Advent and Christmastide with a thousand-year-old poem, one of the earliest recorded in our language.

ADVENT AND EXPECTATION

Advent is a time of expectation. Early Christians such as St. Peter[1] and St. Stephen[2] understood Christ as the fulfillment of Moses' pronouncement that the Lord would "raise up" a prophet who would lead Israel and, through them, the Gentiles. More than this, they proclaimed the Good News that he was not only this prophet, but also the Son of God. Though the Church continues to proclaim this Good News, she also continues to wait for Christ's return at the end of time:

> Until everything is subject to him, "until there be realized new heavens and a new earth in which justice dwells, the pilgrim Church, in her sacraments and institutions, which belong to this present age, carries the mark of this

[1] See Deut 18:15, Acts 3:12–26, esp. 3:22.
[2] See Deut 18:15, Acts 7:2–53, esp. 7:37

world which will pass, and she herself takes her place among the creatures which groan and travail yet and await the revelation of the sons of God". That is why Christians pray, above all in the Eucharist, to hasten Christ's return by saying to him: *Marana tha!* "Our Lord, come!" [I Cor 16:22; Rev 22:17–20]. (*CCC* §671)

As the Church's liturgical tradition grew and deepened through the centuries, a period of double waiting for the Messiah's "advent" (Latin for "coming to") developed before the celebration of the Lord's Nativity. This double expectation placed the liturgical assembly in a rich and stunning double belonging. On the one hand, they took their place among the community of patriarchs and prophets who longed to see the Christ born in the world on Christmas day. On the other, they were also the community of the Church who longs to see Christ "sitting at the right hand of the Mighty One and coming on the clouds of heaven" (Mark 14:62). The balance of readings at Mass and the Liturgy of the Hours during Advent continues to place Christians in this paradoxical position.

The Advent Lyrics (sometimes called *Christ I*) are a witness to this profound longing and were composed by a poet some time in the ninth or tenth century. Though removed from us by language, more than a millennium of history, and (to some extent) artistic sensibility, *The Advent Lyrics* still provide a poignant meditative guide through the dark waiting of Advent and the joyful fulfillment of Christmas. Though from such a long time ago, they share with us a liturgical and spiritual culture focused intently during these seasons on the double expectation of the Incarnation and the *eschaton* (the end of the world) that is ours year after year, until that great Last Day.

THE POEM

When we think of Christian poetry in English, we might think of John Milton's *Paradise Lost* or T. S. Eliot's *Four Quartets*. But Christian poetry in English actually began much earlier than even Milton's day. Around AD 450, members of several Germanic tribes from northwestern Europe settled in Britain. As these newcomers edged out or assimilated the Celtic inhabitants of the island, they created a culture and unified kingdom that we call "Anglo-Saxon England". Anglo-Saxon England became a Christian kingdom throughout the seventh and eighth centuries, with monastic missionaries leading the way and setting a monastic basis for the Church throughout the island.

The Anglo-Saxons started making poems on Christian themes in their own language at least by the late-seventh century, and several volumes of this poetry have come down to us in precious surviving manuscripts. These books were made during a great flowering of learning and the arts in the latter half of the tenth century known as the Anglo-Saxon Benedictine Reform. One of the books produced during this period (*c.* 965–75), the Exeter Book, appears to be the first anthology of English poetry. Though the precise location of its origins remains unclear, the Exeter Book is very likely to have been copied in one of the Reform monasteries or "minsters" in the southwest of England. *The Advent Lyrics* are the first poem in this surprising volume.

The Advent Lyrics form a sequence of short meditations based on what are known as the "O Antiphons". These "O Antiphons" are short poetic texts recited before and after the Marian Canticle (the Magnificat) at the evening office of prayer known as Vespers, from 17 to 23 December. The Roman Rite of the Catholic Church still preserves these antiphons, and several Protestant liturgies employ them as well. In addition to these "Great O Antiphons" familiar to those who celebrate the Liturgy of the Hours, there were also similar antiphons that "traveled along" with the main set during the medieval period—what are now usually called the "Monastic O Antiphons". The poet of *The Advent Lyrics* chose a number of all these antiphons to pore over and elaborate in verse. The poem as it is found in the Exeter Book starts in the middle of a sentence, as a result of at least one page having gone missing, and this, combined with the fact that three of the standard "O Antiphons" are not represented in the poem, has led many to believe that three sections of the poem are currently missing (we include the texts of these three anthems for the reader's reference, even though they are not found in the manuscript).

The brilliance of *The Advent Lyrics* is not found in the regular, sonorous flow of syllables and rhyme matched with penetrating wit that are characteristic of early-modern or Romantic English poetry. Nor is it found in the discerning observation of the minutiae of the human condition and the mind-bending metaphors used by so many contemporary English poets. Instead, our poet wedded early-medieval strategies for interpreting the Scriptures to the ways poets shaped verse in Old English. In doing so, he created a lush sequence permeated by the two great themes of Advent: the (double) coming of the Savior and humanity's great need for divine aid and mercy.

These themes are largely explored through the Christian strategy of interpretation called "typology". To understand *The Advent Lyrics*—and the Church's traditional reading of Scripture and salvation history—we need to spend a moment getting a grasp on what typology is: a strategy for interpreting Scripture used by several writers in the New Testament[3] and emphatically adopted by the Fathers of the Church and their heirs for centuries thereafter. In this way of thinking about Scripture and salvation history,

---

[3]   See for example, I Cor 10:6 and 11; Gal 4:21–31; Rom 5:14; Heb 9:11–10:14; 1 Pet 3:19–22.

the patterns set by events and people in the Old Testament are "fulfilled" by events or people in the New Testament. But—and this is crucial for understanding how typology works—in "fulfilling" these patterns, the New Testament does not dismiss the validity of the Old.

For example, the First Letter of St. Peter tells us that Noah's "ark, in which a few persons, eight in all, were saved through water", "prefigured baptism, which saves you now" (3:20–1). The Christian sacrament of baptism "fulfills" the pattern set up in Genesis through Noah's ark and his family's survival of the Flood. But this "fulfillment" does not mean that Noah's ark is no longer important or necessary, or that it was merely a symbol. The idea is that God set up patterns in the real world, awaiting the fulfillment of them all in his Son's Incarnation and the Church. And it is exactly all these fulfillments of previous patterns that shows how God has been guiding the course of events from the start, that this was his "plan for the fullness of time, to sum up all things in Christ, in heaven and on earth" (Eph 1:10).

This way of talking about the Scriptures can lead to some misunderstanding, so we think a note of caution is desirable at this point. As stated above, the "fulfillment" of typology found in the New Testament does not dismiss the validity of the Old Testament. The Old Testament (overlapping to a large extent with the Hebrew Bible) has its own integrity, cherished by the Jewish people, and early Christians maintained that the Old Testament was inspired precisely because the New Testament did not have the same meaning if the Old Testament was not understood to be the inspired Word of God.[4]

---

[4]   This all means that, though it can sound similar, this way of reading the Scriptures does not participate in what is called "supercessionist theology", a way of doing theology that argues the covenant God made with the Jewish people is somehow "superseded" by the New Covenant established by Jesus at the Last Supper (Luke 22:20). This theology, which did begin early, is not how we see typology used

This typological way of thinking about Scripture and salvation history matters for *The Advent Lyrics* because this vision is how the entire poem is built. For example, throughout the poem, the speakers ("we") switch (sometimes confusingly) between being pre-Incarnation members of the people of God on earth, pre-Incarnation denizens of hell awaiting the Harrowing, and Christians awaiting the Second Coming. There is no contradiction here, though, because the figures of the past are "fulfilled" in the present through typology, creating a profound association of different eras and peoples that simultaneously defies clear distinction. Typology is about abandoning the "either/or" for the "both/and". One of the most interesting elements of the poem is how it brings its own audience into its typological play in just this way.

The great variety of typological associations made by the poet can seem unwieldy to modern sensibilities. Yet the deeper we plunge into the imagination that works typologically, the more the great harmony, depths, and interconnectedness of the Word of God are laid bare. And so, throughout *The Advent Lyrics*, Christ is Melchizedek, the Key of David, and the psalm's "cornerstone", and Mary is the closed gate of Ezekiel's vision (Ezek 44:1–3), a new Eve, and Isaiah's Bride. Medieval exegetes (people who interpret Scripture) considered this kind of "chewing over" of the mysterious connections in Scripture a kind of "rumination": a chewing, swallowing, regurgitating, and re-chewing of the blended whole of the elements the Word of God provides. This rich and careful association of events and persons in salvation history leads the reader into more penetrating contemplation of all the "shadows of those blessings which were still to come" (Heb 10:1).

---

in the New Testament. The Vatican II document *Nostra aetate* finally denounced this view and heartily encourages mutual respect and harmony among Jews and Christians, which we affirm as well.

From this density, the poet of *The Advent Lyrics* shapes a dynamic poem that is at once a lament on unredeemed humanity, a dire call for help and mercy, and a joyous celebration of redemption, salvation, and the culmination of all things before the throne of glory. If we attend to the poem's structure carefully, we see that what might appear at first glance to be static embellishments of antiphons stacked one after another actually forms a movement that reflects a Christ-centered, optimistic vision of reality.

This vision develops in three movements. Sections one through to eight present ruminations securely set before the Incarnation; section nine presents the definitive historical moment of the Incarnation; and sections ten through to twelve position the poem's speakers within the time following the Incarnation but, paradoxically, in a continued state of acute longing and peaceful repose. In this movement we see reflected not just the season of Advent, but the movement of Advent along with Christmastide. After a proportionately very long period of expectation (sections one through to eight) the Christ child is beheld (section nine), after which a brief but joyful period—Christmas through to Epiphany—follows (sections ten through to twelve), during which the Church meditates on the blessings of salvation. The entire sweep also reflects that second expectation, as we hope that a long period of waiting will see at last the coming of Christ at the end of time. For then, "There will be no more night. They will not need the light of a lamp or the light of the sun, for the Lord God will give them light. And they will reign for ever and ever" (Rev 22:5).

THE PRESENT TRANSLATION

Old English verse has its own ways of making poetry, ways that are often strange even to regular readers of modern English poetry. Old English poets delighted in apposition (the restatement of a grammatical unit in new words and without conjunctions) and built the sentences' sense through half-lines rather than full lines, both of which lend a sense of repetition to Old English poetry. In addition, Old English meter is based on stressed syllables. Almost every line has four stressed syllables ("pow-" in "power" is the stressed syllable), two in each half-line. The "beat" between the two half-lines is called a "caesura". The number of unstressed syllables in a line varies widely. This is very different from what many of us learn about English meter in school—Shakespeare's and Wordsworth's iambic pentameter is based on a much more regular stress and syllable pattern. This difference often makes Old English poetry sound "clunky" and "irregular" in comparison to the later tradition on first hearing. Also, alliteration, the repetition of initial sounds in words ("rough" and "ready" alliterate), is the most noticeable sonic element of Old English verse. There is no rhyme. In order to "bind" together the two half-lines in each line of verse, at least one stressed syllable on each side of the caesura needs to alliterate. (There are intricate rules here, but let's not bother with that.) The interplay between stressed syllables and alliteration across the caesura is what makes Old English poetry artful—downright fun to listen to.

I (Jacob) have in no way attempted to follow the rules of Old English meter strictly in the present translation. I have attempted to maintain a fairly regular pattern of stressed syllables and alliteration that reflects to some degree the sound of Old English verse without torturing modern English syntax. Each line has four main stressed syllables (at least as I read them), and a widely fluctuating number of unstressed syllables. I have mostly tried to maintain the caesura, and this produces a noticeably "choppy" effect throughout. The pattern of alliteration is where (as seems inevitable in modern English) I have taken the greatest liberties. While at least two stresses alliterate in almost every single line, the positions of these in the line and even within the word do vary a great deal. In addition, as was the case in Old English verse, any vowel alliterates with any other vowel.

The intent here has been not to slavishly imitate the original in word or meter, but to suggest the rhythm and sonic qualities of Old English verse for those unfamiliar with them, while providing a translation faithful to the original's sense that is readable as a modern English poem. For those who desire greater guidance through the themes, typological references, and structure of the poem, we have included brief comments on these in the "Commentary" sections that follow each section of the poem.

While a translation with commentary can certainly not stand up against the beauties of the Old English in its original context, we hope that the current work can help modern English speakers enjoy this literary jewel from a thousand years ago and lead modern Christians to a prayerful longing for Christ during Advent and throughout their lives.

THE ILLUSTRATIONS

Medieval liturgical and biblical manuscripts often included illustrations to embellish, reinforce, and accent the written word. To imitate this tradition in bookmaking, we have included here visual art that embellishes, reinforces, and accents the formal strategies used in *The Advent Lyrics*. Daniel Mitsui is a contemporary religious artist who possesses a deep respect for medieval art and aesthetics, and we are delighted to have his ink drawings, made entirely by hand on paper, accompany and complement this translation.

The border designs framing the poems are modeled after the "interlace" design common to early Germanic and Celtic art and brought to a particular highpoint, in manuscript illustration, by the Irish and Anglo-Saxon illustrators of the early Anglo-Saxon period. The greatest example of this style is the book known as the Lindisfarne Gospels, written and illustrated probably by Eadfrith, bishop of Lindisfarne, around the year 700. Similarly, the "carpet page" placed at the beginning of this book is a particularly arresting feature of the Lindisfarne Gospels. Its abstract and kaleidoscopic patterning culminate in a cross design. Of these carpet pages, the northern English poet Basil Bunting has said:

> As you gaze at one of these so-called carpet pages, little by little, the confusion of ornament sorts itself out, you notice how carefully balanced the whole thing is, and a great cross emerges from the welter of ornament. There are occasions when the cross is made conspicuous, but usually it requires a good look at the page before you identify the cross. I fancy this must have been Eadfrith's way of implying that if you looked steadily at all the innumerable details which are all we ever see of the world you might detect amongst them a symbol of unity which, for him, was the symbol of Christianity.
>
> What would have astonished later artists of a different tradition is that Eadfrith does not emphasise this cross, or very rarely does. He doesn't force it on the beholder. He leaves him to find it, to discover it for himself, to learn what holds the page together, and discovering it in this way, it stays far more firmly in your mind than a great contrasty cross thrown at you, so to speak.[5]

The complex and intricate designs of such early Anglo-Saxon art have been compared to the "weaving of words" ("wordum wrixlan" in Old English) that is Old English poetry. The half-lines' alliteration that crosses over each line's caesura, the apposition threading stress patterns through lines and phrases, and the verbal echoing all mirror the welter of repetition-with-variation that at first sight (or hearing) often seems like barely controlled chaos and

---

[5]   Basil Bunting, *On Poetry* (Baltimore: The Johns Hopkins University Press, 1999), 12.

that finds a visual parallel in Anglo-Saxon interlace design. Though *The Advent Lyrics* were copied down more than two centuries after the Lindisfarne Gospels were compiled, a similar artistic sensibility informs them both and reinforces the pattern of and means to beauty revealed in these early medieval artistic styles.

THE OLD ENGLISH TEXT

The Old English text of *The Advent Lyrics* given here is from George Philip Krapp and Elliott Van Kirk Dobbie's edition of *The Exeter Book*, used by the kind permission of Columbia University Press. However, the following minor changes have been made: we have added acute accents to indicate long vowels/diphthongs; we have altered the placement of quotation marks in the section "Éalá Ióséph", changing punctuation in 167–8; we have made emendations in lines 6, 19, 22, 23, 31, 58, 70, 86, 152, 153, 188, 291, 340, and 395 based on the commentary in Bernard J. Muir's *The Exeter Anthology of Old English Poetry*, vol. 2; and we have left out the poem's first word ("cyninge"), the remnant of an incomplete line. We have also included the first three Latin antiphons, which are not treated in the poem as it has come down to us. Though it cannot be proved now, these three almost surely were treated in the initial leaves of the manuscript, which are now missing. A further change from the manuscript is the layout of the verse in lines: Old English verse was originally set out as if it was prose (while Latin verse was, indeed, set out in lines). The insular script of the original is imitated in the Old English text given here (but a transcription in modern letters is given as an appendix); some letter forms may be a little unfamiliar, particularly g (ᵹ), r (ꞃ), s (ꞅ), t (ꞇ), and w (ƿ), as well as ð and þ (both = th).

THE ADVENT LYRICS

O WISDOM

O Sapientia, quae ex ore Altissimi prodisti, attingens a fine usque ad finem, fortiter suaviterque disponens omnia: veni ad docendum nos viam prudentiae.

O Wisdom, coming forth from the mouth of the Most High, reaching from one end to the other, mightily and sweetly ordering all things: come and teach us the way of prudence.

[No Old English text survives of O Wisdom.]

O ADONAI

O Adonai et Dux domus Israel, qui Moysi in igne flammae rubi apparuisti, et ei in Sina legem dedisti: veni ad redimendum nos in bracchio extento.

O Adonai and leader of the House of Israel, who appeared to Moses in the fire of the burning bush and gave him the law on Sinai: come and redeem us in your outstretched arm.

[No Old English text survives of O Adonai.]

O ROOT OF JESSE

O Radix Iesse, qui stas in signum populorum, super quem continebunt reges os suum, quem Gentes deprecabuntur: veni ad liberandum nos, iam noli tardare.

O Root of Jesse, who stand as a sign among the peoples, before you kings will shut their mouths, to you the nations will make their prayer: come to deliver us, and delay no longer.

[No Old English text survives of O Root of Jesse.]

I. O KING OF ALL THE NATIONS

O Rex gentium, et desideratus earum, lapisque angularis, qui facis utraque unum: veni, et salva hominem, quem de limo formasti.

O King of all the nations and their desire, O Cornerstone who make both one: come and save humanity, which you fashioned from the dust.

Ðú eart ré peallrtán   þe ðá pýrhtan íu
  pıðpurron tó peorce.   Pel þé geríreð
þæt þú héarod ríe   healle mænne,
ond geromnıge   ríde peallar
færte geróge,   rlınt unbrǽcne,
þæt geond eorðbýrg eall   éagna gerhþe
pundrıen tó porlde   puldrer ealdor.
Gerpeorula nú þurh reanocrǽrt
      þín rýlrer peorc,
róðfært, rıgorbeorht,   ond róna rorlǽt
peall pıð pealle.   Nú ır þám peorce þearr
þæt ré crærtga cume   ond ré cýnıng rýlra,
ond þonne gebéte,   nú gebrornað ır,
húr under hróre.   Hé þæt hrá gercóp,
leomo lǽmena;   nú rceal lírrnéa
þone péngan héap   ppáþum áhreddan,
earme rrom egran,   rrá hé ort dýde.

You are the wall=stone the workers long=past
    rejected from their plans. How perfect it is
that you stand as the head of that radiant hall,
wondrously joining those broadest walls
with strongest joints and fastest stone:
that every city=dweller with eyes to see
will marvel forever at the Lord of might.
Reveal to us now the luminous victory—
your trustworthy work, the truth that keeps
wall against wall. Your work now longs
for her builder to come, the King himself,
and mend its parts, restore its peace,
that brilliant building. He made the body,
the limbs of clay; now the Lord of life
must rescue this mass of wretches from evil,
prostrate in sins, as he did in the past.

COMMENTARY ON LYRIC I

As we begin reading *The Advent Lyrics*, our Anglo-Saxon poet first draws our attention to Christ as a unifying force. We find God "wondrously joining those broadest walls" of the Old Testament and the New through the Incarnation of the Son. The poet also sets up two themes that will appear again and again in his sequence: humanity's wretchedness as we await the Son's coming and our desire for release from this bondage. As he does this, one of his key strategies is to draw us into identifying with the poem's speakers. By bringing us into his poem through the words "we", "us", and "our", he helps us enter into our own wretchedness and need for God's coming (at Christmas as well as at the end of time).

The section itself begins with the image of the "cornerstone" from Psalm 118:22. This was a messianic image for Israel, and Jesus applies the image to his New Covenant. In the synoptic Gospels' parable of the wicked tenants, Jesus describes the tenants' abuse of the vineyard owner's servants and son (Matt 21:33–46; Mark 12:1–12; Luke 20:9–18). When he asks the chief priests and Pharisees what the vineyard owner will do to the tenants, they answer that "He will put those wretched men to a wretched death and lease his vineyard to other tenants who will give him the produce at the proper times". Jesus responds to their answer by drawing the Old Testament and his New Covenant together through the "stone that has been rejected". It is this stone that will become the cornerstone of the new community he will build, and he tells these religious authorities that "the kingdom of heaven will be taken away from you and given to a people that will produce its fruit". This productivity, the Psalmist, Jesus, and the poet all affirm, will be "wonderful in our eyes". This moment, when the kingdom of heaven is given to the Church so that we can begin to bear Christ's fruit, is the blessed moment we await in the unfolding of Advent.

Our poet calls the Church, this building formed "wall against wall", a "radiant hall". And this hall needs Christ to serve as its "head" (see Col 1:18). The section goes on to build Christ up into a glorious figure by praising him as the "Lord of might", the "King", and the "Lord of life". All this draws on traditional Anglo-Saxon heroic imagery based in earthly kings' halls decked with gold and tapestries. But most importantly, this stress on Christ's majesty begins the building of a contrast between him and wretched humanity, dwelling in the shadows of sin and death. Though we might be uncomfortable with this dramatic split between God and humanity, it was common in early-medieval spirituality and is firmly grounded in the cries and praises of the Psalms and Prophets, and the potent supplication of the liturgy.

By the end of the section, however, we turn our gaze to God as the "Lord of life", the creator as builder, who makes Adam (whose name encompasses all humankind) from the earth. The humble description of bodies of clay is actually taken up into the majestic imagery of Christ the King. We are now a vast number of individuals *and* a single body comprised of various parts. We are at once the people of God before the Incarnation, longing for God to descend "like showers watering the earth" (Ps 72:6), *and* the Christian liturgical assembly awaiting the celebration of the Incarnation at Christmas every year.

By this first section's ending, our need and brokenness beg for our maker to come to refashion our sorry state. And we find as the imagery proceeds that the "Lord of life" will not remain a bystander who fixes from outside. The Son will accomplish this "luminous victory" by taking his own place *within* the "radiant hall" as its head: "the Word became flesh, and made his dwelling among us" (John 1:14).

II. O KEY OF DAVID

O Clavis David, et sceptrum domus Israel; qui aperis, et nemo claudit; claudis, et nemo aperit: veni, et educ vinctum de domo carceris, sedentem in tenebris et umbra mortis.

O Key of David and royal power of Israel, who opens and no one closes, who closes and no one opens: come, lead the bound out from prison, those who dwell in darkness and the shadow of death.

Éalá þú reccend ond þú ryht cyning,
sé þe locan healdeð, líf ontyneð,
éadgum upwegas, óþrum forwyrneð
wlitigan wilsiþes, gif his weorc ne déag.
Húru wé for þearfe þás word sprecað,
ond myndgiað þone þe mon gescóp
þæt hé ne léte tó lose weorðan
cearfulra þing, þe wé in carcerne
sittað sorgende, sunnan wénað,
hwonne ús líffréa léoht ontyne,
weorðe ussum móde tó mundboran,
ond þæt tydre gewitt tíre bewinde,
gedó úsic þæs wyrðe, þe hé tó wuldre forlét,
þá wé héanlíce hweorfan sceoldan
on þis enge lond, éðle bescyrede.

    Forþon secgan mæg, sé ðe sóð spriceð,
þæt hé áhredde þá forhwyrfed wæs,
frumcyn fira. Wæs séo fæmne geong,
mægð mánes léas, þe hé him tó méder geceas;
þæt wæs geworden bútan weres frígum,
þæt þurh bearnes gebyrd bryd éacen wearð.
Nænig efenlíc þám, ær ne siþþan,
in worlde gewearð wífes geearnung;
þæt dégol wæs, dryhtnes geryne.
Eal giofu gæstlíc grundsceat geondspreot;

O holy Ruler and right=wise King,
who guards the locks and opens life:
the blessed go upwards, others denied
those wondrous roads if their works lack merit.
Because we need help, we cry out to you —
mindful of him who made humanity —
hear us and save us. Give heed, dear Lord,
to our anxious concern, as we ail here in prison
sitting sorrowful, hoping for sun,
the Lord of life to disclose that light —
a worthy protector of our pining spirits,
weaving with glory our feeble wits:
make us your people, partakers in glory,
since we've had to make this world our home,
this narrow realm, cut off from your reign.
And so we can say, if we speak the truth,
that the Savior rid us of our wrongful customs,
our wretched ways. It was a young woman,
a sinless maiden, he chose for his mother:
Mary conceived without man's embrace.
She swelled with child by the Holy Spirit.
No conception, before or since,
has rivaled hers in the whole world.
That was a mystery, the Mighty One's secret.
His holy gift grew in the world;

þær wirna fela weard inlihted
lare longsume þurh lifes fruman
þe ær under hodman biholen lægon,
witgena wodrong, þa re waldend cwom,
re þe reorda gehwær wyne gemiclad
ðara þe geneahhe noman scyppender
þurh horsene had hergan willað.

every mystery was newly illumined,
the Lord of life's long=held secret,
laying too long hidden in shadow,
the prophet's hints, when the Prince appeared,
revealing the meaning behind every veil
previously hung by God's praisers
who lauded in wisdom his many wonders.

COMMENTARY ON LYRIC II

In contrast with the first section, which brought together and united, this second section of *The Advent Lyrics* begins by providing a warning. Our poet first takes up the "door" imagery implied in the title "Key of David". There is a looming risk after we have encountered the one "who opens and no one closes, who closes and no one opens": the door might be closed. This leads to a frank acknowledgment of the situation: "the blessed go upwards" while those whose "works lack merit" will go by other roads. This is unsettling. Possibly frightening. Or maybe it's easy to skip over this— how often do we really stop to think about the "last things" (death, judgment, heaven, and hell) in our daily lives?

However, note that we do not find a bleak or lurid depiction of the pains and sufferings of hell (those gut-wrenching tirades are more common several centuries later). Rather, we have a stark demand for a response, the wake-up call that is Advent. In the face of such a predicament, we turn to the "holy Ruler and right-wise King", crying out for help, seeing the need for grace before we can even think of "merit" or its lack. We linger in the darkness of our prison awaiting the sun, awaiting the one who can open the locks of salvation, holiness, and joy.

As this section continues, the poet redirects our attention to humanity's need for the Incarnation once again. His strategy this time is to have us (the audience) become more emphatically identified with the Prophets of the Hebrew Bible, who hope for "light" and "sun" in this "narrow realm, cut off from your reign". But this time, to place before us a more concrete hope, the fulfilling of this need comes into view for the first time as the baby growing in Mary's virgin womb: "the Mighty One's secret", the Light of the world growing in darkness. In this child, "every mystery [is] newly illumined" and "every veil" hung by the Prophets in their visions of what was to come is brought into the full light of day. For "in times past, God spoke in partial and various ways to our ancestors through the prophets; in these last days, he spoke to us through a son . . . who is the refulgence of his glory, the very imprint of his being, and who sustains all things by his mighty word" (Heb 1:1–3). Our hope is enkindled as we move from the ominous warning at the section's outset to this assurance of a new light coming into the world.

At this moment the poet of *The Advent Lyrics* brings his readers into his poem more directly, inviting the reader to take on the role of a person caught up in this transitional moment, this point between two worlds, and to embrace his ruminations as a means to spiritual illumination and to becoming "partakers in glory" through the birth of Mary's son.

III. O JERUSALEM

O Hierusalem, civitas Dei summi, leva in circuitu oculos tuos et vide Dominum Deum tuum: ecce iam veniet solvere te a vinculis.

O Jerusalem, city of the great God: lift up your eyes round about, and see your Lord, for soon he will come to release you from your chains.

Éalá ribbe ʒeꞃhð,   ꞃancта Hieꞃuꞃalem,
cynertóla cyrt,   Crírter burʒlonð,
engla éþelrtól,   onð þá áne in þé
ráule róðꝼærтꞃa   rimle ʒenertað,
pulðnum hnémʒe.   Næꝼne pommer тácn
in þám eanðʒeanðe   éapeð peonþeð,
ac þé ꝼinina ʒehpýlc   ꝼeon ábúʒeð,
pænʒðo onð ʒepinner.   Birт тó pulðne ꝼull
hálʒan hýhter,   rrá þú ʒeháтen eart.
Sioh nú rýlꝼa   þe ʒeonð þár rídan ʒerceart,
rpýlce roðoner hnór   rúme ʒeonðplíтan
ýmb healꝼa ʒehpone,   hú þec heoꝼoner cýninʒ
ríðe ʒeréceð,   onð rýlꝼ cýmeð,
nimeð eanð in þé,   rrá hiт ær ʒeꝼýꞃn
píтʒan pírꝼærтe   ponðum ræʒðon,
cýððon Crírter ʒebýnð,   cpæðon þé тó ꝼnóꝼne,
bunʒa beтlícart.   Nú ir þæт beann cýmen,
ápæcneð тó pýnne   peoncum Ebnéa,
bninʒeð blirre þé,   benða onlýꞃeð
niþum ʒenéððe.   Neanoþeanꝼe conn,
hú þé eanma rceal   áne ʒebíðan.

Ovision of peace, pure Jerusalem,
   greatest kingdom and
Christ's royal home —
seat of angels! Only in you
do steadfast souls find fullness of rest,
sharing in wonders! No stain of sin
is found in that homeland,
   hallowed and blessèd —
criminal deeds are kept at bay,
suffering and strife. You are the city
filled with the hope of all the holy ones.
Behold, throughout this whole expanse
under heaven's vault — view its entirety
on every side — see how the King
seeks you in coming, draws near himself,
sets up his tent, as in times past,
as the keen prophets rightly disclosed,
proclaiming Christ's birth as comfort,
finest of cities! Now that Son is come,
solace arisen for Hebrew sorrows,
bringing bliss and breaking bonds
forged in error. He feels their need —
how the helpless await his grace!

COMMENTARY ON LYRIC III

This short section seems straightforward, but it actually draws the poem's audience closer to heaven and to the physical and historical reality of the Incarnation in subtle ways. Here, as in so much of Christian tradition, Jerusalem is the ancient city in Palestine, but it is also so much more.

We begin by speaking to the city, praising its importance in God's plan for his chosen people. It is the "greatest kingdom and Christ's royal home—seat of angels!" The Temple is here. Mt. Zion is here. This is King David's royal city. Following the Church Fathers' explanation of the city's Hebrew name, the poet calls Jerusalem the "vision of peace".

But very quickly, we see that "Jerusalem" takes on new meaning. When the poet says "Only in you do steadfast souls find fullness of rest", it becomes difficult to maintain the idea that we're still talking about the city in Palestine. As we find out that "no stain of sin is found in that homeland" and that it is "the hope of all the holy ones" it appears that we are being led to conclude we're now actually talking about heaven, the "New Jerusalem" found in Revelation. This can be strange, even disconcerting, if we are reading with attention. But the seamless transition from literal city to allegorical name for heaven is exactly how typology (the fulfillment of figures and events of the Old Testament in those of the New Testament and the Church) works. As the poet plays with the meaning of Jerusalem, he takes us along with him, and in this case draws our attention to heaven.

And then the play continues, and we find that we have left the New Jerusalem for somewhere "under heaven's vault". "The King" is seeking Jerusalem, "draws near" and "sets up his tent". But there is a problem—Christ was born in Bethlehem, not Jerusalem. So what is happening? "Jerusalem" has shifted meaning again. As we saw in the last section, Mary has already "conceived without man's embrace; she swelled with child by the Holy Spirit". *She* is the "finest of cities" where "now that Son is come", waiting in the darkness of her womb as we await his grace. The poet uses the scriptural and liturgical language of typology to bring the potent symbol of Jerusalem, Christ's home in heaven, and his new "home" in the Virgin's womb together in one very dense meditation that focuses our attention squarely on the physical reality of the Incarnation.

These densely typological moments in the poem are probably the most difficult for modern readers to pick up on and to fully enter into. But when we pay close attention to the liturgy and to the ways the New Testament interprets the Old, we find this way of thinking everywhere. When we are able to see these connections, how in the mind of the Church the New Testament fulfills elements found in the Old, we begin to see with the Church how God's providential plan "hangs together", how great its unity really is. Christian hope is a faithful expectation that God will fulfill his promises, as he has in the past. This hope is what Advent is all about.

IV. O VIRGIN OF VIRGINS

"O virgo virginum, quomodo, quomodo fiet istud, quia nec primam similem visa es nec habere sequentem?" "Filiae Hierusalem, quid me admiramini? Divinum est misterium hoc quod cernitis."

"O virgin of virgins, how, how can this be? For never was there one like you, nor will there ever be." "Daughters of Jerusalem, why do you look wondering at me? What you behold is a divine mystery."

"Éalá pípa pýnn   ȝeond puldþer þrým,
pæmne fréolícaſt   oþer ealne þoldan ſcéat
þæſ þe æfne rundbúend   reȝȝan hýrdon,
ápece úſ þæt ȝeþýne
    þæt þé oſ þoderum cþóm,
hú þú éacnunȝe   æfne onþenȝe
beaþneſ þurh ȝebýrde,   ond þone ȝebedſcipe
æfteſ monþíran   mód ne cúðeſ.
Ne pé ſóðlíce   ſpýlc ne ȝeþruȝnan
in æþdaȝum   æfne ȝelimþan,
þæt ðú in rundurȝieſe   ſpýlce beþénȝe,
ne pé þæþe þýrde   þénan þurſon
tópeaþd in tíde.   Húþu tþéoſ in þé
peoþðlícu puraðe,   nú þú puldþeſ þrým
bóþme ȝebæþe,   ond nó ȝebþorþað þeaþd
mæȝðhád ſé micla.   Spá eal manna beaþn
ſoþȝum ſáþað,   ſpá eft ſíþað,
cennað tó cpealme."   Cpæð ſío éadȝe mæȝ
ſýmle ſiȝoſeſ full,   ſancta Maſía:
"Hpæt iſ þéoſ þundþunȝ   þe ȝé þáſiað,
ond ȝéomþende   ȝehþum mænað,
ſunu Solimæ   ſomod hiſ dohtoſ?
Fſicȝað þurh fýrþet   hú ic fæmnan hád,
mund minne ȝeheold,   ond éac módoſ ȝepeaþd
mæþe meotudeſ ſuna.   Forþan þæt monnum niſ

"O delight of women amid heaven's wonders,
under welkin's vault the noblest virgin
that sea-dwellers ever heard spoken of:
make known the mystery, the Spirit's miracle,
how you grew and were given the angel's word,
conceived a Son and never knew
a bedmate's warmth, a man's embrace.
Never before had such a feat
occurred on earth, happened under heaven,
a woman conceiving by such special grace;
nor need we expect to see the same
in days to come! Dwelling in you
the Truth shown forth, heaven's refulgence
carried in your womb, and kept you clean,
virginity inviolate. Every person
sows in sorrow, and in turn reaps,
bears fruit in torment."
        Filled with God's grace,
crowned in sanctity, Mary speaks:
"Why are you amazed at this divine marvel,
lamenting as you bewail your woes,
sons of Salem, and daughters too?
Curious, you ask how I continued a virgin,
held my maidenhood and became mother
of the Most High. To human minds

cúð ʒepýne,   ac Cpíſt onppáh
in Dáuiðeſ   ðýppe mæʒan
þæt iſ Éuan ſcyld   eal foppýnðeð,
pæpʒða ápoppen,   ond ʒepulðpað iſ
ſé héanpa háð.   Hýht iſ onfanʒen
þæt nú blétpunʒ mót   bæm ʒemæne,
peſum ond píſum,   á tó populðe foſð
in þám uplícan   enʒla ðſéame
mið ſóðfæðeſ   ſymle punian."

this remains a mystery; yet Christ revealed
to all in David's dear kinswoman
that the guilt of Eve is gone for good,
the curse cast off; the humbler state
stands exalted. Hope is conceived,
that now a blessing may rest on both,
women and men, world without end
in that heavenly joy on high with the angels,
to live triumphantly with the Father of Truth".

Commentary on Lyric IV

This section continues the progression from an abstract thinking about Christ's birth to the physical reality, embodied in the increasing focus on Mary. As the previous section brought our focus literally "down to earth" from the heavenly Jerusalem to Mary's pregnant body, this section questions her directly and brings forth her own voice, putting us in imaginative dialogue with the *Theotokos*, the Mother of God.

As the section begins, we are not the liturgical assembly looking back at the Incarnation, nor are we objective observers at a distance. The poem brings us in close to the marvel of Mary's virgin pregnancy. As the antiphon suggests and Mary herself will inform us in a moment, the speakers here are citizens of "Salem", the previous section's Jerusalem. (This dialogue seems to echo the Old Testament's Song of Songs, in which the "Daughters of Jerusalem" ask questions of the Song's Bride.) When she addresses us as the "sons of Salem, and daughters too", she disarms us, not allowing us to remain abstract speakers without a place or a name. Now *we* are the inhabitants of Jerusalem and those who encounter her and the mysterious reality she bears into our world. We are dumbfounded by Mary's role in salvation history—in humble wonder but also searching curiosity. Echoing Mary's question for Gabriel, we want to know, "How can this be?"

Mary responds to us directly as we try to figure out the mystery, gently chiding us for concerning ourselves "with things too sublime for [us]" (Ps 131:1). Here we enter on God's hidden turf, which can only be accepted in faith, not rationally understood. While she may understand that such curiosity is natural, she points us to what matters, as she always does. For her, the point is not to comprehend the miracle of the Incarnation, but to embrace the fact that Christ has "cast off" the ancient curse, that "hope is conceived", that women and men have received a great blessing, that they may once again "live triumphantly with the Father of Truth".

One literary note: the Anglo-Saxons used seafaring imagery often throughout their poetry, and they regularly refer to "people" generally as people who specifically sail or live on the sea: hence the "sea-dwellers" at the beginning of this lyric who hear of the noble virgin. This metaphor became especially potent when an Anglo-Saxon poet retold the story of Exodus and imagined the Israelites escaping across the Red Sea as Germanic seafaring warriors!

V. O RADIANT DAWN

O Oriens, splendor lucis aeternae et sol iustitiae: veni, et illumina sedentes in tenebris et umbra mortis.

O Radiant Dawn, splendor of eternal light, sun of justice: come, shine on those who dwell in darkness and the shadow of death.

Éalá éarendel,   engla beorhtast,
ofer middangeard   monnum sended,
ond sóðfæsta   sunnan léoma,
torht ofer tunglas,   þú tída gehwane
of sylfum þé   symle inlíhtes!
Spá þú, god of gode   géano ácenned,
sunu sóþan fæder,   swegles in wuldre
bútan anginne   æfre wære,
swá þec nú for þearfum   þín ágen geweorc
bideð þurh byldo,   þæt þú þá beorhtan ús
sunnan onsende,   ond þé sylf cyme
þæt ðú inléohte   þá þe longe ær,
þrosme beþeahte   ond in þéostrum hér,
sæton sinneahtes;   synnum bifealdne
deorc déaþes sceadu   dréogan sceoldan.
Nú wé hyhtfulle   hælo gelýfað
þurh þæt word godes   weorodum brungen,
þe on frymðe wæs   fæder ælmihtigum
efenéce mid god,   ond nú eft gewearð
flæsc firena léas,   þæt séo fæmne gebær
géomrum tó géoce.   God wæs mid ús
gesewen bútan synnum;   somod eardedon
mihtig meotudes bearn   ond sé monnes sunu
geþwære on þéode.   Wé þæs þonc magon
secgan sigedryhtne   symle bí gewyrhtum,
þæs þe hé hine sylfne   ús   sendan wolde.

O shining Light, luminous Angel —
    descending to those dwelling
  on this sad, poor earth —
righteous Ray of our spiritual Sun:
you illumine all times outside of time,
resplendent beyond the stars. As you,
begotten God from God in the glory
of heaven — holy Son of the Father —
ever existed without beginning,
so your own works pray in their weakness
that you might send the gleaming Sun
and come yourself to illumine those lingering
here, covered with smoke and unceasing
night, enduring the shadow of death.
With hope we believe in the light of salvation
won for us all by the Word of God,
co=eternal with the Father from the first —
who now, free of suffering, in flesh,
came from Mary to comfort mourners.
God was seen among us, sinless:
Son of God and Son of man
living in harmony here on the earth.
So we give thanks unceasingly for this wonder:
that the God of victories would give us himself.

COMMENTARY ON LYRIC V

Like a good teacher or preacher, our poet does not want us to grow complacent. Just as the poem begins to take on a concrete setting and present direct speech between more or less concrete people, we once more draw back from the stage of this drama to praise the Son as the "Dawn", "eternal Light", "Sun of justice", all of which will illumine us who dwell in darkness and death's shadow.

In one sense, this section moves us back somewhat, pulling away from our discussion of the virgin birth from Mary to a more abstract statement of humanity's need for Christ's coming among us. But in the larger development of the poem, this "interruption" serves to prolong the tension of waiting as we continue to trust and fail to see what is awaited.

This section also uses the antiphon's light imagery to invite us into contemplation of Christ's divine nature. In contrast with modern Western Christianity's usual focus on Jesus and his earthly ministry, here this "shining Light"[1] and "righteous Ray" illumines "all times outside time" "beyond the stars". This is a view of the grand and overwhelming nature of the divine from a cramped and darkened earthly perspective—our perspective. This perspective need not feel self-condemnatory or overly pessimistic, since through it the poet provides us a space in which to contemplate Christ, "begotten God from God in the glory / of heaven".

---

[1] For all Tolkien fans: this "shining Light" of our title (*Earendel* in Old English) was an early inspiration for J. R. R. Tolkien's mythology of Middle-earth, being included in one of his early poems on Arda (1914) and the name (as Eärendil) of a main character in the earliest story of the mythology, that of *The Fall of Gondolin* (1916–17). See his "Drafts for a Letter to 'Mr. Rang'", *The Letters of J. R. R. Tolkien*, ed. H. Carpenter (London: George Allen & Unwin, 1981), no. 297.

This section is not concerned only with what Christ *becomes* for us, but also shifts our focus onto who he is in himself.

As he draws ever closer to the Incarnation, the poet reminds us, won't let us forget, that this "luminous Angel" who will descend "to those dwelling on this sad, poor earth" is also one who "ever existed without beginning" and is "co-eternal with the Father from the first". This exalted view of Christ "from below" opens up a space for faith and thanksgiving, even as we continue to long for his "descending".

VI. O EMMANUEL

O Emmanuel, Rex et legifer noster, exspectatio gentium et Salvator earum: veni ad salvandum nos, Domine Deus noster.

O Emmanuel, king and lawgiver, desire of the nations, Savior of all peo= ple: come and set us free, Lord our God.

Éalá ȝæꞃꞇa ȝod, hú þú ȝléaplíce
mid noman ꞃyhꞇe nemned ƿæꞃe
Emmánúhél, ſƿá hiꞇ enȝel ȝecƿæð
æꞃeꞃꞇ on Ebꞃéꞃc! Þæꞇ iſ eꝼꞇ ȝeꞃehꞇ,
ꞃúme bí ȝeꞃýnum: "Nú iſ ꞃodeꞃa ƿeaꞃd,
ȝod ꞅýlꝼa mid úſ." Sƿá þæꞇ ȝomele ȝeꝼýꞃn
ealꞃa cýninȝa cýninȝ ond þone clænan éac
ꞃácend ꞃódlíce ꞃæȝdon ꞇópeaꞃd,
ſƿá ſé mæꞃa íu, Mélchiꞃédech,
ȝléap in ȝæꞃꞇe ȝodþꞃým onꝩꞃáh
éceꞃ alpaldan. Sé ƿær æ bꞃinȝend,
láꞃa lædend, þám lonȝe hiſ
hyhꞇan hideꞃcýme, ſƿá him ȝeháꞇen ƿær,
þæꞇꞇe ꞅunu meoꞇudeꞃ ꞅýlꝼa polde
ȝeꝼælꞅian ꝼoldan mæȝðe,
ꞃƿýlce ȝꞃundaſ éac ȝæꞃꞇeꞃ mæȝne
ꞃíþe ȝeꞃécan. Nú híe ꞃóꝼꞇe þæꞃ
bídon in bendum hꝩonne beaꞃn ȝodeſ
cꝩóme ꞇó ceaꞃiȝum. Foꞃþon cꝩædon ſƿá,
ꞃúꞃlum ȝeꞃlæhꞇe: "Nú þú ꞅýlꝼa cum,
heoꝼoneꞃ héahcýninȝ. Bꞃinȝ úꞅ hælolíꝼ,
péꞃiȝum píꞇeþéopum, pópe ꝼoꞃcýmenum,
biꞇꞃum bꞃýneꞇéaꞃum. Iſ ꞅéo bóꞇ ȝelonȝ
eal æꞇ þé ánum heꞃ ꝼoꞃ oꝼeꞃþeaꞃꝼum.
Hæꝼꞇaꞃ hýȝeȝéompe hideꞃ ȝeꞃeceſ;

O God of spirits: so sagely and wisely
      have you been named
   with that holy Name,
Emmanuel, as the angel announced
first in Hebrew, freely interpreted
in its hidden sense as "Now heaven's Guard,
God, is with us." As the ancients foretold
the blessed coming of the King of kings,
so the priest Melchizedek in days long past,
the goodly priest, revealed God's glory,
the Lord of all. He brought the Law,
gave them learning, those who for so long
hoped for his appearance, as they were promised:
that the Son of God himself would come
and cleanse the world and those who kept it,
seek too in the strength of the blessèd Spirit
the earth's very depths. Now,
   mildly they've endured,
suffering in bonds, 'til the Son of God
should come for those consumed in cares.
Cringing in torments, they say, "Come now
high King of heaven: bring us healing,
weary and tormented; stem our weeping
with bitter burning tears.
   You are the balm we need;

ne læt þé behindan,   þonne þú heonan cynne,
mænigo þur micle,   ac þú miltse on úr
gecýð cynelice,   Crist neriende,
puldres æþeling,   ne læt ápyngde ofer úr
onpald ágan.   Læf úr écne geféan
puldres þines,   þæt þec peorðien,
peoroda puldorcyning,   þá þú geporhtes ær
hondum þinum.   Þú in héannissum
punast pideferh   mid paldend fæder."

only in you alone do we find our ease!
Seek out these slaves, sad and sorrowful,
and don't leave us behind
    when you leave from here,
this teeming multitude, but have mercy on us.
Come forth as our King, Christ our Savior,
noble and illustrious, nor let the accursed one
rule us again! Grant us gladness
in your worthy glory, that we may worship you,
the Lord of hosts, whom your hands have made,
fashioned long since. You abide forever,
dwelling in the heights
    with the Father of holiness".

COMMENTARY ON LYRIC VI

Like the last section, this meditation extends the period of waiting, this time ruminating on Christ as "King of kings", lawgiver, teacher, purifier. One facet of this rumination that could well benefit from some explanation is when the poet draws our attention to the comparison of Christ to Melchizedek in Hebrews 6:19–7:28. There, the New Testament author explains how Christ's sacrifice is a universal and eternal sacrifice, drawing on the priest Melchizedek's appearance to Abraham in Genesis 14:18–20. Melchizedek is the King of Salem, appears mysteriously, offers bread and wine in worship to "God most high", blesses Abraham and God, and then withdraws just as mysteriously. Drawing on the only other mention of Melchizedek in the Old Testament, the author of Hebrews applies Psalm 110's claim that "You are a priest forever in the manner of Melchizedek" to Christ himself. In doing so, he shows how Christ's priesthood fulfills the Law with its Levitical priesthood and Temple sacrifices. In this priesthood's sacrifice of bread and wine, "a better hope is introduced, through which we draw near to God" (Heb 7:19). Though this may seem like a lot of trouble from an obscure reference in Scripture, Christ's priesthood according to the order of Melchizedek is proclaimed in the Roman Canon of the Mass as well, before the New Covenant's bread and wine are offered to the Father.

Amidst our "step back" from the immediacy we had with Mary's speech to the daughters and sons of Jerusalem in section four, we are offered a new perspective on this section's desire for Christ to "Come now" by listening in on someone else's plea. In the second half of this section, the poet introduces a group of speakers whose voice we can "listen to" and whom we can observe relating to Christ. As these speakers beg Christ to come to relieve their sorrows (a desire we have heard spoken several times now), our minds are directed toward it in a new light, and its urgency is renewed precisely in our temporary removal from it.

VII. O JOSEPH

O Ioseph, quomodo credidisti quod antea expavisti? Quid enim? In ea natum est de Spiritu Sancto e quem Gabrihel annuncians Christum esse venturum.

O Joseph, why did you believe what previously frightened you? Why indeed? Christ, whom Gabriel announced would come, was born in her of the Holy Spirit.

"Éalá Ioséph mín,   Iácóber bearn,
 mæᵹ Dáuíder,   mæran cyninᵹer,
nú þú fréode rcealt   rærte ᵹedǽlan,
álǽtan lufan míne!   Ic lunᵹre eam
déope ᵹedréfed,   dóme bereafod."
"Forðon ic porn for þé   porde hæbbe
rídra ronᵹa   ond rárcpida,
hearmer ᵹehýred,   ond mé horp rrrecað,
torrporda fela."   "Ic téарar rceal
ᵹéotan ᵹéomormod.   God éaþe mæᵹ
ᵹehǽlan hyᵹeronᵹe   heortan mínre,
áfréfran fearceaftne."   "Éalá fǽmne ᵹeonᵹ,
mæᵹð María!   Hpæt bemurnert ðú,
cleopart ceaniᵹende?   Ne ic culpan in þé,
incan ǽniᵹne,   ǽfre onfunde,
pomma ᵹeporhtra,   ond þú þá pord rrricert
rrá þú rýlfa ríe   rýnna ᵹehpylcre
firena ᵹefýlled.   Ic tó fela hæbbe
þær býrdrcýрer   bealpa onfónᵹen!
Hú mæᵹ ic láðiᵹan   láþan rrръéce,
oþþe ondrpare   ǽniᵹe findan
práþum tópiþere?   Ir þæt píde cúð
þæt ic of þám torhtan   temple drýhtner
onféᵹ fréolíce   fǽmnan clǽne,
pomma léаre,   ond nú ᵹehpýrfed ir

MARY:

"Joseph, kin to David the king.
Joseph, you son of Jacob. Suddenly,
without warning you've laid aside our love.
Your decision strips me of sacred honor,
awash in woes since you cast me off".

JOSEPH:

"It's been too much. More reproach and abuse
than I can bear. Bitter stories,
insults and sorrow—so many words!"

MARY:

"I've cried over this strife, my spirit
sobbing, grief=stricken. And yet our God
can heal my heart and comfort your hurts."

JOSEPH:

"My young virgin Mary, are you
the one who grieves, going about
mourning and mingling my shame
    with your own?
I didn't look for your lies, never suspected
your terrible sin. But your tears and your talk
ring hollow, your heart gloats over my grief.
I've taken it all over my chin for this child!
What can I say to their slights, the slander
that follows me, befouling at every turn?

þurh náþƿylcer man. Mé nápþer déaȝ,
recȝe ne rríȝe. Gif ic ȝód srrece,
þonne rceal Dáuíder   dohtor rƿeltan,
stánum ártyrred. Gén rtrenȝre ir
þæt ic morþor hele;   rcyle mánrrara,
láþ léoda ȝehþám   lifȝan riþþan,
frracoð in folcum." Ðá réo fǽmne onprráh
ryhtȝerýno,   ond þur reordade:
"Sóð ic recȝe   þurh runu meotuder,
ȝǽrta ȝéocend,   þæt ic ȝén ne conn
þurh ȝemæcrcipe   monner óþer,
ǽnȝer on eorðan,   ac mé éaden pearð,
ȝeonȝre in ȝeardum,   þæt mé Gabrihél,
heofoner héaȝenȝel,   hǽlo ȝebodade.
Sæȝde róðlíce   þæt mé rƿeȝler ȝǽrt
léoman onlýhte,   rceolde ic lífer þrým
ȝeberan, beorhtne runu,   bearn éacen ȝoder,
torhter tírfruman. Nú ic hir tempel eam
ȝefremed bútan fácne,   in mé frófre ȝǽrt
ȝeeardode. Nú þú ealle forlǽt
ráre rorȝceare. Saȝa écne þonc
mǽrum meotoder runu

   þæt ic hir módor ȝeþearð,
fǽmne forð reþéah,   ond þú fæder cpeden
populdcund bí þéne;   rceolde pítedóm
in him rylfum béon   róðe ȝefylled."

I went to the Temple, received a woman.
Everyone said how spotless she was.
All is done now and I'm left in the dark:
speaking? silence? This is no choice.
Speaking means David's daughter must die,
be slain with stones. Silence then?
Concealing the crime only spreads the sin."
Then Mary opened up that august mystery:
"Listen, you son of Jacob: for this Son,
eternal God, not once did I give
myself to a man's passionate embrace.
Gabriel offered this girl his 'Ave',
told me the tactics of the Holy Spirit:
giving me Light, I would bring forth Life,
the great Son of God and Source of glory.
He's made me his Temple, formed without fault,
a palace for the Paraclete,
   a sanctuary for the Spirit.
And so leave off your lamentation!
Speed your thanks to the dazzling Son
of the everlasting Maker, since I am his mother,
avowed a virgin though fully fruitful,
and you his faithful father! This God
comes in person to make good his prophecies."

COMMENTARY ON LYRIC VII

This section of the poem pulls us back down to the concrete personal level. Here is the most intimate encounter between speakers in the entirety of *The Advent Lyrics*. We become a fly on the wall in the home of Joseph and Mary during a heated conversation. While it is difficult to know precisely where in the infancy narratives of Matthew and Luke this discussion could occur, the poet was surely not asserting that this is what "actually happened". Rather, the poet plumbs Joseph's doubt and the resolution to a tremendously trying situation. The conversation's human pathos and relatability remind us that these two great saints were once two newlyweds trying to figure out their new life together.

Mary finds it difficult to understand how Joseph can have such reluctance regarding the situation she so humbly accepted ("Be it done to me according to your word!"). Joseph, on the other hand, has reservations that we can probably sympathize with. His very human view of the dilemma and his doubt are set against Mary's confident trust that all is well.

Ultimately, Mary exhorts Joseph to stop his lamenting and accept the child as God's since she has been told "the Spirit's tactics" and been made a "palace for the Paraclete". We are not given his response. This omission invites us to fill in what the dialogue lacks — what would our reaction be to the bare physical fact of the Incarnation? How do we react when God's providence crushes our human expectations and undercuts our human institutions? These are just a couple of the questions offered us by this disarmingly intimate view of the Holy Family at its very beginning.

VIII. O KING OF PEACE

O Rex Pacifice, tu ante saecula nate, per auream egredere portam, redemptos tuos visita, et eos illuc revoca, unde ruerunt per culpam.

O King of Peace, you who were born before all ages: come out by the golden gate; visit them you have redeemed, and lead them back to that place from which they fell by sin.

Éalá þú róða   ond þú ribruma
eal ra cyninga cyning,   Crist ælmihtig,
hú þú ær þære   eallum geworden
populde þrymmum   mid þinne puldorfæder
cild ácenned   þurh his cræft ond meaht!
Nis æniȝ nú   eorl under lyfte,
recȝ rearoþoncol,   tó þær spíðe ȝléap
þe þæt árecȝan mæȝe   rundbúendum,
áreccan mid ryhte,   hú þé rodera peard
æt frymðe ȝenom   him tó fréobearne.
Þæt þær þára þinȝa   þe hér þéoda cynn
ȝefruȝnen mid folcum   æt fruman ærest
ȝeporden under polcnum,   þæt pitiȝ ȝod,
lífes ordfruma,   léoht ond þýstro
ȝedælde dryhtlíce,   ond him þær dómes ȝepeald,
ond þá píran abéad   peoroda ealdor:
"Nú ríe ȝeporden forþ   á tó pídan féore
léoht, líxende ȝeféa,   lifȝendra ȝehpám
þe in cnéorissum   cende peorðen."
Ond þá róna ȝelomp,   þá hit spá sceolde,
léoma léohtade   léoda mæȝþum,
torht mid tunȝlum,   æfter þon tída biȝonȝ.
Sylfa rette   þæt þú runu þære
efeneardiȝende   mid þinne énȝan fréan
ærþon óht þisses   æfre ȝepurde.

O you true and, yes, peace=loving Prince,
King of kings, Christ the Almighty:
before all else you existed,
before the multitudes, with your Father,
a Child begotten in his craft and power!
There's no person here beneath the heavens,
subtle of thought and sufficiently wise,
who can say aright to sea=dwellers,
expound properly how heaven's Prince
took you to himself as his treasured Child.
The kin of Adam came to know this,
heard it proclaimed early on:
under the welkin divine Wisdom,
the Lord of life, light and darkness
wondrously parted in his power of judgment,
the Mighty One commanded wisely:
"Now let there be, a steadfast blessing,
light for every living creature
ever to be born as generations abound."
And it happened at once, just as it ought:
the light shone forth on the families of nations,
resplendent among the stars
     through the circuit of hours.
He established that you, his Son,
should dwell together with the only God,

Þú eart séo snyttro   þe þás sídan gesceaft
mid þí waldende   worhtes ealle.
Forþon nis ænig þæs horsc,
   ne þæs hygecræftig,
þe þín fromcyn mæge   fíra bearnum
sweotule geseþan.   Cum, nú, sigores weard,
meotod moncynnes,   ond þíne miltse hér
arfæst ýwe!   Ús is eallum néod
þæt wé þín meðrencynn   mótan cunnan,
ryhtgerýno,   nú wé areccan ne magon
þæt fæðrencynn   sien ówihte.
Þú þysne middangeard   milde geblissa
þurh ðinne hercyme,   hælende Crist,
ond þá gyldnan geatu,   þe in geardagum
ful longe ær   bilocen stódan,
heofona heahfréa,   hát ontýnan,
ond úsic þonne geséce   þurh þín sylfes gong
eaðmód tó eorþan.   Ús is þínra árna þearf!
Hafað sé áwyrgda   wulf tóstenced,
déor dædscúa,   dryhten, þín éowde,
wíde tówrecene.   Þæt ðú, waldend, ær
blóde gebohtes,   þæt sé bealofulla
hýneð heardlíce,   ond him on hæft nimeð
ofer usse níoda lust.   Forþon wé, nergend, þé
biddað geornlíce   bréostgehýgdum

before any of this ever occurred.
You, holy Wisdom, made this wide world,
wrought it all with the Almighty.
And so there's none so sagacious or perceptive
that they can declare clearly to all
the nature of your origin. Come now,
   Author of victory,
King of humanity: show us your mercy,
compassion, and pity! Placate our longing
to know the lineage of your loving mother,
that flawless mystery, for no longer can we figure
your Father's line any further.
Mercifully, you gladden
   this gloom=bound world
in your holy Advent, healing Savior.
Command the golden gates to open,
high Prince of heaven, which in distant pasts
stood fast=locked for the longest time.
Seek us and save us, when you yourself come
humbly to earth — we need your help!
The accursèd wolf has completely scattered
your sheep, blessèd One;
   that shadow=dwelling beast
deeply divided us. What you, divine master
bought with your blood, the baleful enemy

þæt þú hrædlíce helpe gefremme
wérgum wreccan, þæt sé witer bona
in helle grund héan gedréore,
ond þín hondgeweorc, hæleþa scyppend,
móte áwísan ond on ryht cuman
tó þám upcundan æþelan ríce,
þonan ús ær þurh synlust sé swearta gæst
forteah ond forcylde, þæt wé, tíwes þone,
á bútan ende sculon ermþu dréogan,
bútan þú úsic þon oforthcor, éce dryhten,
æt þám léodsceaþan, lifgende god,
helm ælþihta, hreddan wille.

oppresses terribly, taking us captive
against our souls' longing. And so, Savior,
we pray earnestly in our inmost thoughts
that you will swiftly send us your aid,
that the slayer who torments us tearful exiles
in the abyss of hell may fall, humiliated,
and your hands' work, world Creator,
might at last arise and come rightly
to that divine and virtuous kingdom
from which the dark spirit seduced and deceived
those he found reluctant, robbed us of glory,
that we, for all eternity, would suffer torment
unless, with greater speed, eternal God,
from this land's enemy, living Lord,
you should desire to save us, Savior of all!

COMMENTARY ON LYRIC VIII

Notice how, every time the poet draws us into the human drama of the Incarnation, he sends us flying back up to the heights of heaven's secrets. In this section we are again concerned with the co-eternal nature of the Son before creation—that the Son is not a "creature" made by the Father but God without qualification. The Son's role in creation is elaborated upon before our own call for him to come to save us once again rings out, this time set against Satan's wolfish and terrible tricks.

The wonder expressed at this section's outset returns us to the imagery of light. The poet first brings together the source of created light on the first day of creation (Gen 1:3) and the image of God's Wisdom, drawing from Proverbs 3:19 ("The LORD by wisdom founded the earth") and Wisdom's powerful description of herself in Proverbs 8:22–30:

> The LORD begot me, the beginning of his works,
>   the forerunner of his deeds of long ago;
> From of old I was formed,
>   at the first, before the earth ...
> When he established the heavens, there was I,
>   when he marked out the vault over the face of the deep ...
> When he fixed the foundations of the earth,
>   then was I beside him as artisan.
>   (Prov 8:22–3, 27, 29–30)

As we have seen before, beholding Christ in his distant glory as the Son leads us to urge him to "Come" down to our world. We enter into the repeated and dynamic call of Advent—"Come!"—as the poem moves back and forth between heaven and earth.

But in this pivotal section, which leads into our brief glimpse of the Christ child in the section following, the poet continues to pile on images in ways he has avoided until now. Because of this, here the poem becomes somewhat dense, but if we will take the time to sit with these two new images, their poignancy emerges. Deep breath:

The first of the new images is the "golden gate". We beg Christ to "come humbly to earth" and "open" that gate "which in distant pasts / stood fast-locked for the longest time". The "closed gate" begins to resonate if the reader's mind returns to the Key of David and the wall-stone we have already encountered, while its "golden" color echoes the light imagery we have seen so many times. But the "closed gate" also refers more directly to the gate mentioned in the vision of Ezekiel 44:1–2:

> Then he brought me back to the outer gate of the sanctuary facing east, but it was closed. The LORD said to me: This gate must remain closed; it must not be opened, and no one should come through it. Because the LORD, the God of Israel, came through it, it must remain closed.

The gate's closure in Ezekiel's vision refers on the *literal* level to the Lord's return to the restored Temple and his permanent presence there, but on the *typological* level, the closed gate refers not to an architectural feature but to other passageways. One typological gate is Mary's body in the virgin birth. But because these gates "stood fast-locked for the longest time" and they lead to a "divine and virtuous kingdom", the poet might also be relating them to the gate of heaven or of Paradise. Both would fit well; thankfully, one perk of typology means never having to choose only one!

The final image of the wolf creates a greater urgency as we make a final plea for salvation. The poem keeps putting off our arrival at the Incarnation, and the plea for salvation becomes more dire and vivid as we go along. In the closing movement of this section, we become the sheep in Christ's parable of the Good Shepherd, threatened by the wolf and at risk of being devoured unless the "world Creator" saves us from the "shadow dwelling beast", the "baleful enemy", the "slayer", the "dark spirit".

On the sea-dwellers of line 8 of this lyric, see the discussion in the commentary to Lyric IV.

IX. O LADY OF THE WORLD

*O mundi Domina, regio ex semine
orta, ex tuo iam Christus processit
alvo tamquam sponsus de thalamo,
hic iacet in praesepio qui et sidera regit.*

O Lady of the world, sprung of royal
seed: from your womb Christ came
forth, as a bridegroom from his cham=
ber; he lies in a manger who also rules
the stars.

Éalá þú méra middangeardes
séo clǽneste cwén ofer eorþan
þára þe gewurde tó wídan féore
hú þec mid ryhte ealle reordberend
hátað ond secgað, hǽleð geond foldan,
blíþe móde, þæt þú brýd síe
þæs sélestan swegles bryttan.
Swylce þá hýhstan on heofonum éac,
Crístes þegnas, cweþað ond ringað
þæt þú síe hlǽfdige hálgum meahtum
wuldorweoruder, ond woruldcundra
háda under heofonum, ond helpara.
Forþon þú þæt ána ealra monna
geþohtest þrymlíce, þrísthýcgende,
þæt þú þinne mægðhád meotude brohtes,
sealdes bútan sýnnum. Nán swylc ne cwóm
ǽnig óþer ofer ealle men,
brýd béaghroden, þe þá beorhtan lác
tó heofonháme hlútre móde
sibban sende. Forðon héht sigores fruma
his héahbodan hider gefléogan
of his mægenþrymme ond þé meahta spéd
snúde cýðan, þæt þú sunu dryhtnes
þurh clǽne gebýrd cennan sceolde
monnum tó miltse, ond þé, María, forð

O you splendor of the earthly sphere,
you cleanest queen in all creation
born among nations since time's beginning:
everyone able to speak aptly
names you and calls you, among numerous peoples,
glad of mind, the glorious bride
of the most excellent Master of all.
Likewise, those highest in heaven announce,
the servants of Christ, proclaim and sing
that you are the Lady, of lasting virtue,
over the heavenly host, those who hold the world,
dwellers under the sky, and the denizens of hell.
For you alone of all humanity
bravely decided, bold in spirit,
to offer your maidenhood to the Almighty,
incurring no sin. No other will come,
another like you — no woman among mortals,
no ring=adorned bride who can ever render
to our celestial home such a sublime offering
with a pure heart. The Prince of victory
commanded Gabriel, his archangel, to come
from the mighty throng to earth to make known
his supernal strength, that the Lord's dear Son
would be brought into the world, in cleanest birth,
as succor to mankind, and you, Mary, henceforth

efne unƿemme á gehealdan.

    Éac pé þæt gefrugnon, þæt gefýnn bí þé
ródfæst rægde rum pódbopa
in ealddagum, Éraíar,
þæt hé pæne gelæded þæt hé lífer gerteald
in þám écan hám eal rcéapode.
Plát þá rpá pírfært pítga geond þéodland
oþþæt hé gertanode þæn gertaþelad pær
æþelíc ingong. Eal pær gebunden
déopan rince dupu onmǽte,
pundunclommum beþpíþen. Pénde rpíðe
þæt æniʒ elda æfne ne meahte
rpá færtlice fonercýttelrar
on écnerre ó inhebban,
oþþe ðær ceartenhlíder clúrton onlúcan,
æn him goder enʒel þunh glædne geþonc
þá píran onppáh ond þæt pond ácpæð:
"Ic þé mæʒ recʒan þæt ród gepeanð
þæt ðár gýldnan gatu gíet rume ríþe
god rýlf pile gærter mægne
gefælran, fæden ælmihtiʒ,
ond þunh þá færtan locu foldan néoran,
ond hio þonne æften him éce rtondað
rimle ringaler rpá beclýred
þæt næniʒ óþen, nýmðe nenʒend god,
hý æfne má eft onlúceð."

would ever be held always immaculate.
We've heard more: that long ago, Mary,
a steadfast prophet said concerning you,
in ancient days, dear Isaiah,
that he was brought to the abode of life
and beheld everything in that eternal home.
The prophet gazed beyond this peopled realm
'til he perceived where the precious entrance
was regally couched. Completely bound
in dear treasure was that massive door,
wound with strange bands. He sensed surely
that no one among men at any time
could ever force up such firm fore=bolts
or unlock that city=gate's sturdy latches,
before the angel of God with a gracious mind
explained the matter, a divine message:
"I can tell you what will occur,
how the eternal Father, in God's own time,
our God himself, through these golden gates
will pass in time by the Spirit's power.
Through these indelible locks he'll visit the earth,
and turning back they'll continue to stand
forever and always eternally closed,
that only the Lord might unlock them."
Now the prophet's report is properly fulfilled,
what the holy one saw in hallowed vision.

Nú þæt ir ȝefylled þæt ré fróda þá
mid éaȝum þær on plátade.
Þú eart þæt pealldor, þurh þé paldend fréa
æne on þar eorðan út ríðade,
ond efne rpá þec ȝemétte,
   meahtum ȝehrodene,
clæne ond ȝeconene, Crírt ælmihtiȝ.
Spá ðé æfter him enȝla þéoden
eft unmæle ælcer þinȝer
hopucæȝan biléac, lífer brytta.
íopa úr nú þá áre þe ré enȝel þé,
ȝoder rpelboda, Gabriél brohte.
Húru þær biddað burȝrittende
þæt ðú þá frófre folcum cýðe,
þinne rýlfre runu. Siþþan pé mótan
ánmódlíce ealle hýhtan,
nú pé on þæt beapn foran bréortum rtapiað.
Gebinȝa úr nú þrírtum pordum
þæt hé úr ne læte lenȝ ópihte
in þirre déaððene ȝedpolan hýran,
ac þæt hé úric ȝeferȝe in fæder ríce,
þær pé ronȝléare riþþan mótan
puniȝan in puldre mid peoroda ȝod.

You are the door the divine Ruler
swiftly coursed through when he came
    to us sinners.
Even so, he found you, with virtues for finery,
elect and clean, Christ almighty.
And after his passage the angels' Chief,
the Giver of life, locked with limbs' key
your blessed body against any blemish.
Now show us the grace that God's messenger,
brilliant Gabriel, brought here to you.
On account of this dignity,
    we abject city=dwellers
pray you give solace to every people,
your only Son. We are obliged,
each and every, to rejoice with one accord,
now that we behold our God
    before your breasts.
Pray for us now with holy petitions,
that he not leave us here any longer
in this valley of death to heed the Deceiver,
but convey us speedily to the heavenly kingdom
where we might dwell in dearth of sorrow,
live in glory with the God of hosts.

COMMENTARY ON LYRIC IX

Though the next section will return to pleading for Christ to "hear the call of us wretched captives" and to "come to us yourself", this section presents to our view the historical climax of the poem, the Incarnation of Christ at Bethlehem.

It begins by addressing Mary. But this is no longer the Mary of the seventh section who frets and talks pensively with Joseph. This Mary is a triumphant and regal Mary, the "glorious bride", the "Lady" "of those in heaven and on earth and under the earth" (Phil 2:10). She is exalted in a way similar to Christ's exaltation in previous sections, as a person aflame in the glorified reality of heaven, waiting eagerly to assist the poor captives on earth. She is human, yet she is also unique, and so accorded tremendous praise.

The image of the "golden gates" returns here and now refers to the Virgin herself in ways that were not clear in the eighth section. The poet elaborates this image more than any other in the poem, and appropriately so, since the Virgin as "golden gates" and "closed gate" enables Christ to enter into the world and humanity to access heaven in his grace. (Note: the poet here mistakes "Ezekiel's" vision for "Isaiah's"—the days before easy reference books and search engines!) Ending this description of Christ's entrance into the world through Mary's perpetual virginity, we once again plead that she "show us the grace that God's messenger, / brilliant Gabriel, brought here to you". On this earth, we are never done pleading for Mary to show us her Son.

In the poet's most artistically brilliant and evocative move in the whole poem, we descend from the heights of heavenly imagery to the climax of the poem's theme and the liturgical season. Finally, we "rejoice with one accord" as our yearning is fulfilled: "we behold our God before [her] breasts". A stark and tender image dramatically draws our attention from the grandeur of Mary the Queen of Heaven to the poor new mother, nursing her vulnerable newborn as the world watches in quiet joy — the great and humble paradox of the Incarnation illustrated with consummate and touching artistry, preparing our hearts and minds for Christmas.

X. O LORD OF THE HEAVENS

O Coelorum Domine, qui cum Patre sempiternus es una cum Sancto Spiritu, audi tuos famulos; veni ad salvandum nos, iam noli tardare.

O Lord of the heavens, you who are co=eternal with the Father and one with the Holy Spirit, listen to your servants: come and save us, and do not delay.

Éalá þú hálȝa heofona dryhten,
þú mid fæder þinne ȝefyrn ƿære
efenƿyrcende in þám æþelan hám.
Næs ǽniȝ þá ȝíet enȝel ȝeƿorden,
ne þæs miclan mæȝenþrymmes nán
ðe in roderum up ríce biƿitiȝað,
þéodnes þrýðȝesteald ond his þeȝnunȝa,
þá þú ǽrest ƿære mid þone écan fréan
sylf settende þár sídan ȝesceaft,
bráde brytenȝrundas. Bǽm inc is ȝemǽne
héahȝǽst hléofæst. Ƿé þé, hǽlend Críst,
þurh éaðmédu ealle biddað
þæt þú ȝehýre hæfta stefne,
þínra níedþíowa, nerȝende god,
hú ƿé sind ȝeƿencte þurh úre sylfra ȝeƿill.
Habbað ƿræcmæcȝas ƿérȝan ȝǽstas,
hetlen helsceaþa, hearde ȝenýrƿad,
ȝebunden bealorápum. Is séo bót ȝelonȝ
eall æt þé ánum, éce dryhten.
Hréoƿceariȝum help, þæt þín hidercyme
áfréfre féasceafte, þéah ƿé fæhþo ƿið þec
þurh firena lust ȝefremed hæbben.
Ára nú onbehtum ond usse yrmþa ȝeþenc,
hú ƿé tealtriȝað týdran móde,
hƿearfiað héanlíce. Cým nú, hæleþa cyninȝ,

O you holy Lord of the heavens,
from the world's foundation you dwelt
with the Father
equal in being in that supernal abode.
No angel yet existed at all,
not one of those greatest ethereal troops
who oversee that seraphic kingdom,
the Ruler's retinue and regal dwelling,
when you were at first with the wondrous Father,
yourself establishing the spacious world,
the broad expanses. From out of you both
proceeds the Paraclete. We pray to you, Christ,
in all humility, holy Savior,
that you hear the call of us wretched captives,
your enslaved creatures, saving God,
how we are wounded by our own wills.
Hostile spirits, accused hell=fiends,
have constrained your suffering outcasts,
bound us balefully. Our only balm
is you alone, eternal Lord.
Help us in our sorrows, come to us yourself,
to comfort us paupers, though we've caused a feud,
revolted against you in our vile desires.
Have mercy on your servants,
remember our miseries,

ne lata tó lange.   Úr iſ hirra þearf,
þæt þú úſ áhredde   ond úſ hælogiefe
ródfæſt ſýlle,   þæt þé ribban fonð
þá ſellan þing   ſýmle móten
geþéon on þéode,   þinne ƿillan.

how we stumble, faint of spirit,
wandering care=worn. Come now, our King,
don't delay too long! We long to see your grace,
that you'd rescue us all, grant your radiant
healing and truth, that we henceforth
might ever prefer the better part,
choose and perform your perfect will.

COMMENTARY ON LYRIC X

From the exultant and tender rollercoaster of the ninth section, here we once again return to the praise of Christ as co-eternal with the Father and the captives' need for deliverance from their torment. In this section, Christ's Incarnation in history is set within a meditation on the Trinity's eternity. It is as if the poet feels an urgency to remind us of God's absolute transcendence and glory just as soon as his vulnerability is finally made manifest in his human birth.

While this may seem like backtracking, it is perfectly in line with liturgical time. From the view of eternity Christ is always born and always glorified. From our perspective of the Church on earth, he is also always in the process of coming. In this section, we see this in how we once again become the "wretched captives . . . wounded by our own wills". But we also see it even more acutely in our awareness of ourselves as actually awaiting his Second Coming at the end of time in our own lives.

The poet here calls to mind that we are always waiting in a place of tension where Christ's saving work "is already present in mystery" yet remains "to be fulfilled 'with power and great glory' by the King's return to earth" (CCC §669 and 671).

XI. O TRINITY

O beata et benedicta et gloriosa Trini-
tas, Pater et Filius et Spiritus Sanctus,
te iure laudant, te adorant, te glori-
ficant omnes creaturae tuae, O beata
Trinitas.

O beatific and blessèd and glorious
Trinity, Father and Son and Holy Spirit,
rightly do all your creatures praise you,
adore you, and glorify you, O blessed
Trinity!

Éala seo wlitige, weorðmynda full,
heah ond halig, heofoncund þrynes,
brade geblissad geond brytenwongas
þa mid ryhte sculon reordberende,
earme eorðware ealle mægene
hergan healice, nu us hælend god
wærfæst onwrah þæt we hine witan moton.
Forþon hy, dædhwæte, dome geswiðde,
þæt soðfæste seraphinnes cynn,
uppe mid englum a bremende,
unaþreotendum þrymmum ringað
ful healice hludan stefne,
fægre feor ond neah. Habbað folgoþa
cyst mid cyninge. Him þæt Crist forgeaf,
þæt hy motan his ætwiste eagum brucan
simle singales, swegle gehyrste,
weorðian waldend wide ond side,
ond mid hyra fiþrum frean ælmihtigne
onsyne wreoð, ecan dryhtnes,
ond ymb þeodenstol þringað georne
hwylc hyra nehst mæge ussum nergende
flihte lacan friðgeardum in.
Lofiað leoflicne ond in leohte him
þa word cweþað, ond wuldriað
æþelne ordfruman ealra gesceafta:

O flawless Beauty, blessed and glorious,
  exalted and holy, heavenly Trinity,
who are boldly blessed in this earthly abode:
those able to speak must ably give praise,
those dwelling on earth, with all their power,
humbly laud you. Now loving God,
reveal the Savior so we might receive him.
So those vigorous saints, crowned in splendor,
that steadfast kin of six=winged seraphim,
the angels on high, ever exulting,
sing out and on with untiring strength
sweetly from far and near, full=throated
and most exaltingly! The choicest office
they hold for the King, and Christ granted it:
that they might enjoy his presence
    with their own eyes,
forever unceasingly, celestially adorned,
worship their Lord in heaven's wide ways.
With their wings the God of wonders'
face they conceal, the supernal Lord's,
and about that throne they zealously throng,
to see which might fly nearest the Savior
and soar closest to those peaceful courts.
They laud their Beloved, and in his light
they sing these words in streaming glory

"Hálig eart þú, hálig,   héahengla brego,
ród rígoner fréa,   rímle þú birt hálig,
dryhtna dryhten!   Á þín dóm wunað
eorðlic mid ældum   in ælce tíd
wíde geweorþad.   Þú eart weoroda god,
forþon þú gefyldest   foldan ond rodoras,
wígendra hléo,   wuldres þínes,
helm alwihta.   Sie þé in héannessum
éce hælo,   ond in eorþan lof,
beorht mid beornum.   Þú geblétsad léofa,
þe in dryhtnes noman   dugeþum cwóme
héanum to hróþre.   Þé in héahþum síe
á bútan ende   éce herenis."

to the Lord of origins, of all creation:
"Holy are you, holy, Ruler most high,
you are ever holy, enduring Prince,
Lord of hosts! Your glory lasts
everywhere on earth, in every time,
truly honored. You are God of troops,
you eternally uphold the heavens and the earth,
Defender of warriors, with your faithful glory,
Helm of all creatures.

    Throughout the celestial heights
may glory be yours, praise of God,
bright among men. May you be blessed,
who in the Name of the Lord came
    to those lowly ones,
solace to the wretched. May rightful benediction
be to you in every height, ever without end."

COMMENTARY ON LYRIC XI

This second-to-last section continues our reflection on the nature of God in his glory and Trinity. Yet now we move from pleading for Christ to come to joyful thanksgiving for his coming at Christmas, and we leave the O Antiphons of Advent behind.

The almost unceasing focus here is on the Trinity and its praise by humanity but more especially by the choirs of angels. Calling to mind the joy of the heavenly host who sang before the shepherds on Christmas night (Luke 2:8–15), we hear the "Holy! Holy! Holy!" chanted as the seraphim flit about the divine presence in their "choicest office", recalling the vision of Isaiah in the divine throne room (Isa 6:3). As the seraphim continue their praise, they draw our minds (and God's) briefly back to the great saving act of the Incarnation as they end their praise with the Messianic cry, "Blessed is he who comes in the name of the Lord!" (Matt 21:9).

The angels remind us of the biblical and liturgical turf we are on and have been on throughout the entire poem, and how the great events of the past and the present, and even the exaltation of the living God in his highest courts, all relate to his greatest and most bewildering act: his descent on Christmas night. Let us join their holy choirs with praise and thanksgiving (see Heb 13:15).

XII. O WONDERFUL EXCHANGE

O admirabile commercium, Creator generis humani animatum corpus sumens, de Virgine nasci dignatus est: et procedens homo sine semine, largitus est nobis suam deitatem.

O wonderful exchange: the Creator of humanity, assuming a living body, deigned to be born of the Virgin and, becoming human without seed, has given us his divinity.

Éalá hwæt, þæt is wræclic wrixl   in wera life,
þætte moncynnes   milde scyppend
onféng æt fæmnan   flæsc unwemme,
ond sío weres friga   wiht ne cúþe,
ne þurh sæd ne cwóm   sigores ágend
monnes ofer moldan;   ac þæt wæs má cræft
þonne hit eorðbúend   ealle cúþan
þurh geryne,   hú hé, wodera þrym,
heofona héahfréa,   helpe gefremede
monna cynne   þurh his módor hrif.
Ond swá forðgongende   folca nergend
his forgifnesse   gumum tó helpe
dǽleð dógra gehwám,   dryhten weoroda.
Forþon wé hine dómhwate   dǽdum ond wordum
hergen holdlíce.   Þæt is héalic rǽd
monna gehwylcum   þe gemynd hafað,
þæt hé symle oftost   ond inlocast
ond geornlicost   god weorþige.
Hé him þære lisse   léan forgildeð,
sé gehálgoda   hǽlend sylfa,
efne in þám éðle   þær hé ǽr ne cwóm,
in lifgendra   londes wynne,
þær hé gesǽlig   siþþan eardað,
ealne widan feorh   wunað bútan ende. Ámén.

O wondrous exchange in this weary life:
humanity's merciful Shaper received
humanity from his immaculate mother
while she was ignorant of man's embrace.
The King of victory, he did not come
from human seed — a greater skill
than men can know was at work in that mystery:
the Glory of heaven, the Lord on high,
sent aid to us all through his mother's womb.
And, so proceeding, the Savior daily
and graciously offers his forgiveness to us.
For this we praise him with sincere piety
in our words and our deeds. We do our best
while here, wounded in the world, to worthily
and earnestly and frequently honor our God.
The hallowed Lord, the loving Savior,
will grant his disciple his gift of salvation,
bringing that laborer to the land of the living
where the blessèd abide eternally. Amen!

Commentary on Lyric XII

In this closing section, our poet presents us with a meditation boldly proclaiming the divinization of humanity that Christ's Incarnation makes possible. As St. Athanasius famously put it, "the Son of God became man so that we might become God". Paradoxically, this most radical of claims is presented in a relatively restrained tone.

To underscore for us that everything has been changed by this one long-awaited event, the poet trains our gaze on the "commerce" between heaven and earth provided by the Son's Incarnation. This harks back to the opening section's meditation on Christ as "the head of that radiant hall, / wondrously joining those broadest walls" of the Old and New Testaments, of heaven and earth. But the poet also returns our attention to the *cause* of this commerce: our minds and hearts are once again pointed toward Christ's condescension in the Incarnation, its manifestation in the Virgin Birth, and its saving power.

Rather than go off to the heavens in flights of exaltation as he does in sections ten and eleven, here our poet keeps us firmly grounded on the earth in all but the last few lines. We have pleaded throughout the poem for Christ's coming to free us from bondage in death's shadow, and here at last is a calm but confident claim that this is indeed what Christ has accomplished and what he continues to offer: "the Savior daily / and graciously offers his forgiveness to us". In return, we can only "praise him with sincere piety / in our words and our deeds. We do our best / while here" though we are "wounded in the world". Across a millennium, this final assessment still rings true.

We have here a sober and grateful acknowledgment of Christ's salvific work. And yet, even as we end on a restrained note in contrast to the last several sections' more jubilant praise, the poet cannot simply leave us on the earth to go about our business—even in a transformed world. In the closing few lines, we shift our gaze once more and finally toward the heavenly life and beatific vision, as our poet calmly but expectantly assures us that "the loving Savior" will bring the "laborer" who has sought to honor him "to the land of the living / where the blessèd abide eternally".

Here at the last, *The Advent Lyrics* is a poem that, in imitation of the liturgy itself, marshals the vast store of inspired poetic associations found throughout the Scriptures, the commentaries on the Scriptures, and the Church's Tradition to end in a measured tone that nonetheless directs us—heart, mind, body, soul, and spirit—to our eternal resting place with "the hallowed Lord". *Marana tha!*

SMALL-GROUP DISCUSSION GUIDE

As noted in the introduction, one origin of this book was in the enthusiastic response Jacob received from sharing two Old English poems with a small group for fathers in his family of parishes in Milwaukee, Wisconsin. Since we are looking to share this literary treasure from the deep tradition of the Church with a broader audience, we thought it would be helpful to provide a basic framework for reading *The Advent Lyrics* with a small group.

The following guides provide basic outlines and questions for a four-meeting session of a small group that intends to read *The Advent Lyrics* together as a way to deepen their experience of the liturgical seasons of Advent and Christmastide. They can of course be changed in any way as one may see fit. In fact, we encourage anyone interested in doing so to adapt, rearrange, add, or subtract whatever they think would make these materials more effective for their unique groups.

Advent Lyrics Small Group: ideally for 3–12 people; four sessions, to be ideally held twice during the weeks of Advent, once immediately before or immediately after Christmas, and once between Christmas and Epiphany; set up to have one or two people leading the group with others invited to engage in conversation. Though not necessary, if leaders want to find trustworthy supplemental materials regarding Anglo-Saxon England, Anglo-Saxon Christianity and monasticism, and Old English literature, see Further Reading for initial suggestions.

SESSION 1. LYRICS I–III.
FIRST OR SECOND WEEK OF ADVENT

Opening prayer. Extemporaneous or prepared prayer calling on the Holy Spirit for guidance during your time together.

Introductory questions. Choose one or more of the following to invite the group into discussion.

◆ How do you usually relate to Advent as a season in the liturgical year?

◆ What is the main reason you were interested in joining this reading group, and what do you hope to take from our time together?

Background. Using the introduction to this book, explain the very basic historical context of the poem and what the poem is like (for example: define "Anglo-Saxon England"; define "Old English"; focus on describing how the different sections move the reader through Advent to Christmas and toward Epiphany; note that the poet uses "typology" and briefly explain what typology is by using some of the examples in the introduction).

Reading. Read the sections yourself or invite a group member to read.

Discussion questions. After reading, choose one or more of the following questions to invite the group into more focused discussion on what the poem says to them.

◆ What parts (passages, images, or individual words) of the poem stand out to you?

◆ Can you identify with the poem's speakers (the poem's "we")? Are there moments where this is easier or harder? Why?

◆ How do you read these sections' overall tone—is the beginning of the poem hopeful? intimidating? strange? comfortable? intimate?

Closing prayer. Extemporaneous or prepared prayer thanking God for your time together and blessings on your journeys through Advent.

SESSION 2. LYRICS IV–VI.
THIRD OR FOURTH WEEK OF ADVENT

Opening prayer. Extemporaneous or prepared prayer calling on the Holy Spirit for guidance during your time together.

Introductory questions. Choose one or more of the following to invite the group into discussion.

◆ How are you "keeping" Advent?

◆ Can you describe a challenge you have in preparing your heart and mind for Christ's coming at Christmas?

Context. Briefly summarize the basic content of last week's reading and note that this week's readings are still set before the Incarnation at Christmas.

Reading. Read the sections yourself or invite a group member to read.

Discussion questions. After reading, choose one or more of the following questions to invite the group into more focused discussion on what the poem says to them.

◆ How has the tone of the sections changed from last week's reading to this week's?

◆ As Mary chides "us" for prying into the mystery of her miraculous pregnancy and the Incarnation, she shadows Gabriel's response to her own question of understanding ("How can this be, since I have no relations with a man?") when "she was greatly troubled" (Luke 1:29, 34). As he told her that "nothing will be impossible for God", she invites us into her "fiat" ("May it be done to me") as she dismisses our questioning. Is our Advent spent in surrendering to God's mystery in the Incarnation, or seeking out more and more explanations of or distractions from this central mystery of the Faith?

Closing prayer. Extemporaneous or prepared prayer thanking God for your time together and blessings on your journeys through Advent.

SESSION 3. LYRICS VII–IX.
IMMEDIATELY BEFORE OR AFTER CHRISTMAS

Opening prayer. Extemporaneous or prepared prayer calling on the Holy Spirit for guidance during your time together.

Introductory questions. Choose one or more of the following to invite the group into discussion.

◆ Can you recall a time when you weren't placing all your trust in God?

◆ How will you (or how did you) celebrate Christmas?

Context. Briefly summarize the movement of the first two weeks, and then note that this week the poem comes to one climax as it briefly gives us a glimpse of the Incarnation with the Christ child nursing at Mary's breasts.

Reading. Read the sections yourself or invite a group member to read.

Discussion questions. After reading, choose one or more of the following questions to invite the group into more focused discussion on what the poem says to them.

◆ In the seventh section, do you find yourself identifying with Mary or Joseph more? Why?

◆ In the eighth section, how does Satan's sudden appearance as a wolf and enemy make you think differently of "our" repeated pleas for Christ to come to earth?

◆ The ninth section is filled with imagery for Mary—which image draws your attention the most?

Closing prayer. Extemporaneous or prepared prayer thanking God for your time together and blessings on your journeys through Advent.

SESSION 4. LYRICS X–XII.
BETWEEN CHRISTMAS AND EPIPHANY

Opening prayer. Extemporaneous or prepared prayer calling on the Holy Spirit for guidance during your time together.

Introductory questions. Choose one or more of the following to invite the group into discussion.

◆ Christ is always with us, but he is also continuously revealed. Can you describe a time during (any) Christmas when Christ was revealed to you in a new way?

◆ Are you still celebrating Christmas in your home? The festival of the Christmas season lasts until the Baptism of the Lord!

Context. Review the basic "movements" of the last three sets of readings, then preview that this week's readings take place after the Incarnation and as Christ is being revealed in new ways (to the shepherds in the fields at night, to the Magi, etc.), which imitates the liturgy's movement from Christmas to Epiphany and the Baptism of the Lord.

Reading. Read the sections yourself or invite a group member to read.

Discussion questions. After reading, choose one or more of the following questions to invite the group into more focused discussion on what the poem says to them.

◆ Why does the poem still ask for Christ to come to relieve us, if Christ has already come in last week's reading? (Note for leaders: consider Epiphany, the Second Coming, and so forth)

◆ How do these final sections "resolve" the poem's action? Do they leave us feeling like the poem is "over"?

◆ Consider the great "exchange" of the Incarnation, what this whole poem has been trying to focus our attention on—in what ways does this belief (what St. Paul called a "stumbling block" and "foolishness" from human perspectives) challenge the choices we make in our day-to-day lives? How do we live in its light?

Closing Prayer. Extemporaneous or prepared prayer thanking God for your time together and blessings on your journeys through Advent.

Further Reading

Æthelwold of Winchester. *The Old English Rule of St. Benedict with Related Old English Texts*. Translated by Jacob Riyeff. Kalamazoo, MI: Cistercian Publications, 2017.

Boenig, Robert. *Anglo-Saxon Spirituality: Selected Writings*. New York: Paulist Press, 2000.

Burlin, Robert B. *The Old English Advent: A Typological Commentary*. New Haven: Yale University Press, 1968.

Campbell, Jackson J. *The Advent Lyrics of the Exeter Book*. Princeton, NJ: Princeton University Press, 1959.

Cavill, Paul. *Anglo-Saxon Christianity: Exploring the Earliest Roots of Christian Spirituality in England*. London: Harper Collins, 1999.

Danielou, Jean. *From Shadows to Reality: Studies in the Biblical Typology of the Fathers*. London: Burns & Oates, 1960.

Delanty, Greg, and Michael Matto. *The Word Exchange: Anglo-Saxon Poems in Translation*. New York: WW Norton, 2011.

Fulk, R. D., and Christopher M. Cain. *A History of Old English Literature*. Malden, MA: Blackwell Publishing, 2005.

Irving, Edward B., Jr. "The Advent of Poetry: *Christ I*". *Anglo-Saxon England* 25 (1996): 123–34.

Krapp, George Philip, and Elliott Van Kirk Dobbie, eds. *The Exeter Book*. New York: Columbia University Press, 1936.

Muir, Bernard, ed. *The Exeter Anthology of Old English Poetry: An Edition of Exeter Dean and Chapter MS 3501*. 2 vols. Exeter: University of Exeter Press, 1994.

Niles, John D. *God's Exiles and English Verse: On the Exeter Anthology of Old English Poetry*. Exeter: Exeter University Press, 2019.

Rankin, Susan. "The Liturgical Background of the Old English Advent Lyrics: A Reappraisal", in *Learning and Literature in Anglo-Saxon England*, ed. Michael Lapidge and Helmut Gneuss. Cambridge: Cambridge University Press, 1985, 317–40.

Ward, Benedicta. *Christ within Me: Prayers and Meditations from the Anglo-Saxon Tradition*. Kalamazoo, MI: Cistercian Publications, 2008.

—— *High King of Heaven*. Kalamazoo, MI: Cistercian Publications, 1999.

Webster, Leslie. *Anglo-Saxon Art*. Ithaca, NY: Cornell University Press, 2012.

The Old English Text
in Modern Transliteration

I

Ðú eart sé weallstán　þe ðá wyrhtan íu
wiðwurpon tó weorce.　Wel þé geríseð
þæt þú héafod síe　healle mǽrre,
ond gesomnige　síde weallas
fæste gefóge,　flint unbrǽcne,
þæt geond eorðbyrg eall　éagna gesihþe
wundrien tó worlde　wuldres ealdor.
Gesweotula nú þurh searocræft　þín sylfes weorc,
sóðfæst, sigorbeorht,　ond sóna forlǽt
weall wið wealle.　Nú is þám weorce þearf
þæt sé cræftga cume　ond sé cyning sylfa,
ond þonne gebéte,　nú gebrosnad is,
hús under hrófe.　Hé þæt hrá gescóp,
leomo lǽmena;　nú sceal líffréa
þone wérgan héap　wráþum áhreddan,
earme from egsan,　swá hé oft dyde.

II

Éalá þú reccend　ond þú riht cyning,
sé þe locan healdeð,　líf ontýneð,
éadgum upwegas,　óþrum forwyrneð
wlitigan wilsíþes,　gif his weorc ne déag.
Húru wé for þearfe　þás word sprecað,
ond myndgiað　þone þe mon gescóp
þæt hé ne lǽte　tó lose weorðan
cearfulra þing,　þe wé in carcerne
sittað sorgende,　sunnan wénað,
hwonne ús líffréa　léoht ontýne,
weorðe ussum móde　tó mundboran,
ond þæt týdre gewitt　tíre bewinde,

gedó úsic þæs wyrðe,   þe hé tó wuldre forlét,
þá wé héanlíce   hweorfan sceoldan
tó þis enge lond,   éðle bescyrede.
    Forþon secgan mæg,   sé ðe sóð spriceð,
þæt hé áhredde   þá forhwyrfed wæs,
frumcyn fira.   Wæs séo fǽmne geong,
mægð mánes léas,   þe hé him tó méder gecéas;
þæt wæs geworden   bútan weres frígum,
þæt þurh bearnes gebyrd   brýd éacen wearð.
Nǽnig efenlíc þám,   ǽr ne siþþan,
in worlde gewearð   wífes gearnung;
þæt dégol wæs,   dryhtnes gerýne.
Eal giofu gǽstlíc   grundscéat geondspréot;
þǽr wísna fela   wearð inlíhted
láre longsume   þurh lífes fruman
þe ǽr under hoðman   biholen lǽgon,
wítgena wóðsong,   þá sé waldend cwóm,
sé þe reorda gehwæs   rýne gemiclað
ðára þe geneahhe   noman scyppendes
þurh horscne hád   hergan willað.

III

Éalá sibbe gesihð,   sancta Hierusalem,
cynestóla cyst,   Crístes burglond,
engla éþelstól,   ond þá áne in þé
sáule sóðfæstra   simle gerestað,
wuldrum hrémge.   Nǽfre wommes tácn
in þám eardgearde   éawed weorþeð,
ac þé firina gehwylc   feor ábúgeð,
wærgðo ond gewinnes.   Bist tó wuldre full
hálgan hyhtes,   swá þú geháten eart.
Sioh nú sylfa   þe geond þás sídan gesceaft,
swylce rodores hróf   rúme geondwlítan
ymb healfa gehwone,   hú þec heofones cyning
síðe geséceð,   ond sylf cymeð,
nimeð eard in þé,   swá hit ǽr gefyrn
wítgan wísfæste   wordum sægdon,
cýðdon Crístes gebyrd,   cwǽdon þé tó frófre,
burga betlícast.   Nú is þæt bearn cymen,
áwæcned tó wyrpe   weorcum Ebréa,
bringeð blisse þé,   benda onlýseð
níþum genédde.   Nearoþearfe conn,
hú sé earma sceal   áre gebídan.

IV

"Éalá wífa wynn geond wuldres þrym,
fǽmne fréolícast ofer ealne foldan scéat
þæs þe ǽfre sundbúend secgan hýrdon,
árece ús þæt gerýne þæt þé of roderum cwóm,
hú þú éacnunge ǽfre onfenge
bearnes þurh gebyrde, ond þone gebedscipe
æfter monwísan mód ne cúðes.
Ne wé sóðlíce swylc ne gefrugnan
in ǽrdagum ǽfre gelimpan,
þæt ðú in sundurgiefe swylce befénge,
ne wé þǽre wyrde wénan þurfon
tóweard in tíde. Húru tréow in þé
weorðlícu wunade, nú þú wuldres þrym
bósme gebǽre, ond nó gebrosnad wearð
mægðhád sé micla. Swá eal manna bearn
sorgum sáwað, swá eft rípað,
cennað tó cwealme." Cwæð sío éadge mǽg
symle sigores full, sancta María:
"Hwæt is þéos wundrung þe gé wáfiað,
ond géomrende gehþum mǽnað,
sunu Solimǽ somod his dohtor?
Fricgað þurh fyrwet hú ic fǽmnan hád,
mund mínne geheold, ond éac módor gewearð
mǽre meotudes suna. Forþan þæt monnum nis
cúð gerýne, ac Críst onwráh
in Dáuídes dýrre mǽgan
þæt is Éuan scyld eal forpynded,
wærgða áworpen, ond gewuldrad is
sé héanra hád. Hyht is onfangen
þæt nú blétsung mót bǽm gemǽne,
werum ond wífum, á tó worulde forð
in þám uplícan engla dréame
mid sóðfæder symle wunian."

V

Éalá éarendel, engla beorhtast,
ofer middangeard monnum sended,
ond sóðfæsta sunnan léoma,
torht ofer tunglas, þú tída gehwane
of sylfum þé symle inlíhtes!
Swá þú, god of gode géaro ácenned,

sunu sóþan fæder,   swegles in wuldre
bútan anginne   ǽfre wǽre,
swá þec nú for þearfum   þín ágen geweorc
bídeð þurh byldo,   þæt þú þá beorhtan ús
sunnan onsende,   ond þé sylf cyme
þæt ðú inléohte   þá þe longe ǽr,
þrosme beþeahte   ond in þéostrum hér,
sǽton sinneahtes;   synnum bifealdne
deorc déaþes sceadu   dréogan sceoldan.
Nú wé hyhtfulle   hǽlo gelýfað
þurh þæt word godes   weorodum brungen,
þe on frymðe wæs   fæder ælmihtigum
efenéce mid god,   ond nú eft gewearð
flǽsc firena léas,   þæt séo fǽmne gebær
géomrum tó géoce.   God wæs mid ús
gesewen bútan synnum;   somod eardedon
mihtig meotudes bearn   ond sé monnes sunu
geþwǽre on þéode.   Wé þæs þonc magon
secgan sigedryhtne   symle bí gewyrhtum,
þæs þe hé hine sylfne ús   sendan wolde.

VI

Éalá gǽsta god,   hú þú gléawlíce
mid noman ryhte   nemned wǽre
Emmánúhél,   swá hit engel gecwæð
ǽrest on Ebrésc!   Þæt is eft gereht,
rúme bí gerýnum: "Nú is rodera weard,
god sylfa mid ús."   Swá þæt gomele gefyrn
ealra cyninga cyning   ond þone clǽnan éac
sácerd sóðlíce   sægdon tóweard,
swá sé mǽra íu,   Mélchisédech,
gléaw in gǽste   godþrym onwráh
éces alwaldan.   Sé wæs ǽ bringend,
lára lǽdend,   þám longe his
hyhtan hidercyme,   swá him geháten wæs,
þætte sunu meotudes   sylfa wolde
gefǽlsian   foldan mǽgðe,
swylce grundas éac   gǽstes mægne
síþe gesécan.   Nú híe sófte þæs
bidon in bendum   hwonne bearn godes
cwóme tó cearigum.   Forþon cwǽdon swá,
súslum geslǽhte: "Nú þú sylfa cum,
heofones héahcyning.   Bring ús hǽlolíf,

wérigum wíteþéowum,   wópe forcymenum,
bitrum brynetéarum.   Is séo bót gelong
eal æt þé ánum   her for oferþearfum.
Hæftas hygegéomre   hider geseces;
ne lǽt þé behindan,   þonne þú heonan cyrre,
mænigo þus micle,   ac þú miltse on ús
gecýð cynelíce,   Críst nergende,
wuldres æþeling,   ne lǽt áwyrgde ofer ús
onwald ágan.   Lǽf ús écne geféan
wuldres þínes,   þæt þec weorðien,
weoroda wuldorcyning,   þá þú geworhtes ǽr
hondum þínum.   Þú in héannissum
wunast wídeferh   mid waldend fæder."

VII

"Éalá Ióséph mín,   Iácóbes bearn,
mæg Dáuídes,   mǽran cyninges,
nú þú fréode scealt   fæste gedǽlan,
álǽtan lufan míne!   Ic lungre eam
déope gedréfed,   dóme beréafod."
"Forðon ic worn for þé   worde hæbbe
sídra sorga   ond sárcwida,
hearmes gehýred,   ond mé hosp sprecað,
tornworda fela."   "Ic téaras sceal
géotan géomormod.   God éaþe mæg
gehǽlan hygesorge   heortan mínre,
áfréfran feasceaftne."   "Éalá fǽmne geong,
mægð María!   Hwæt bemurnest ðú,
cleopast cearigende?   Ne ic culpan in þé,
incan ǽnigne,   ǽfre onfunde,
womma geworhtra,   ond þú þá word spricest
swá þú sylfa síe   synna gehwylcre
firena gefylled.   Ic tó fela hæbbe
þæs byrdscypes   bealwa onfóngen!
Hú mæg ic ládigan   láþan sprǽce,
oþþe ondsware   ǽnige findan
wráþum tówiþere?   Is þæt wíde cúð
þæt ic of þám torhtan   temple dryhtnes
onféng fréolíce   fǽmnan clǽne,
womma léase,   ond nú gehwyrfed is
þurh náthwylces man.   Mé náwþer déag,
secge ne swíge.   Gif ic sóð sprece,
þonne sceal Dáuídes   dohtor sweltan,

stánum ástyrfed.   Gén strengre is
þæt ic morþor hele;   scyle mánswara,
láþ léoda gehwám   lifgan siþþan,
fracoð in folcum."   Þá séo fǽmne onwráh
ryhtgerýno,   ond þus reordade:
"Sóð ic secge   þurh sunu meotudes,
gǽsta géocend,   þæt ic gén ne conn
þurh gemǽcscipe   monnes ówer,
ǽnges on eorðan,   ac mé éaden wearð,
geongre in geardum,   þæt mé Gabrihél,
heofones héagengel,   hǽlo gebodade.
Sægde sóðlíce   þæt mé swegles gǽst
léoman onlýhte,   sceolde ic lífes þrym
geberan, beorhtne sunu,   bearn éacen godes,
torhtes tírfruman.   Nú ic his tempel eam
gefremed bútan fácne,   in mé frófre gǽst
geeardode.   Nú þú ealle forlǽt
sáre sorgceare.   Saga écne þonc
mǽrum meotodes sunu   þæt ic his módor gewearð,
fǽmne forð seþéah,   ond þú fæder cweden
woruldcund bí wéne;   sceolde wítedóm
in him sylfum béon   sóðe gefylled."

VIII

Éalá þú sóða   ond þú sibsuma
ealra cyninga cyning,   Críst ælmihtig,
hú þú ǽr wǽre   eallum geworden
worulde þrymmum   mid þínne wuldorfæder
cild ácenned   þurh his cræft ond meaht!
Nis ǽnig nú   eorl under lyfte,
secg searoþoncol,   tó þæs swíðe gléaw
þe þæt ásecgan mǽge   sundbúendum,
áreccan mid ryhte,   hú þé rodera weard
æt frymðe genom   him tó fréobearne.
Þæt wæs þára þinga   þe hér þéoda cynn
gefrugnen mid folcum   æt fruman ǽrest
geworden under wolcnum,   þæt witig god,
lífes ordfruma,   léoht ond þýstro
gedǽlde dryhtlíce,   ond him wæs dómes geweald,
ond þá wísan abéad   weoroda ealdor:
"Nú síe geworden forþ   á tó wídan féore
léoht, líxende geféa,   lifgendra gehwám
þe in cnéorissum   cende weorðen."

Ond þá sóna gelomp,   þá hit swá sceolde,
léoma léohtade   léoda mǽgþum,
torht mid tunglum,   æfter þon tída bigong.
Sylfa sette   þæt þú sunu wǽre
efeneardigende   mid þínne éngan fréan
ǽrþon óht þisses   ǽfre gewurde.
Þú eart séo snyttro   þe þás sídan gesceaft
mid þí waldende   worhtes ealle.
Forþon nis ǽnig þæs horsc,   ne þæs hygecræftig,
þe þín fromcyn mǽge   fíra bearnum
sweotule geséþan.   Cum, nú, sigores weard,
meotod moncynnes,   ond þíne miltse hér
árfæst ýwe!   Ús is eallum néod
þæt wé þín médrencynn   mótan cunnan,
ryhtgerýno,   nú wé áreccan ne mǽgon
þæt fædrencynn   fier ówihte.
Þú þisne middangeard   milde geblissa
þurh ðínne hércyme,   hǽlende Críst,
ond þá gyldnan geatu,   þe in geardagum
ful longe ǽr   bilocen stódan,
heofona héahfréa,   hát ontýnan,
ond úsic þonne geséce   þurh þín sylfes gong
éaðmód tó eorþan.   Ús is þínra árna þearf!
Hafað sé áwyrgda   wulf tóstenced,
déor dǽdscúa,   dryhten, þín éowde,
wíde tówrecene.   Þæt ðú, waldend, ǽr
blóde gebohtes,   þæt sé bealofulla
hýneð heardlíce,   ond him on hæft nimeð
ofer usse níoda lust.   Forþon wé, nergend, þé
biddað geornlíce   bréostgehygdum
þæt þú hrædlíce   helpe gefremme
wérgum wreccan,   þæt sé wítes bona
in helle grund   héan gedréose,
ond þín hondgeweorc,   hǽleþa scyppend,
móte árísan   ond on ryht cuman
tó þám upcundan   æþelan ríce,
þonan ús ǽr þurh synlust   sé swearta gǽst
fortéah ond fortylde,   þæt wé, tíres wone,
á bútan ende   sculon ermþu dréogan,
bútan þú úsic þon ofostlícor,   éce dryhten,
æt þám léodsceaþan,   lifgende god,
helm alwihta,   hreddan wille.

IX

Éalá þú mǽra   middangeardes
séo clǽneste   cwén ofer eorþan
þára þe gewurde   tó wídan féore
hú þec mid ryhte   ealle reordberend
hátað ond secgað,   hǽleð geond foldan,
blíþe móde,   þæt þú brýd síe
þæs sélestan   swegles bryttan.
Swylce þá hýhstan   on heofonum éac,
Crístes þegnas,   cweþað ond singað
þæt þú síe hlǽfdige   hálgum meahtum
wuldorweorudes,   ond worldcundra
háda under heofonum,   ond helwara.
Forþon þú þæt ána   ealra monna
geþohtest þrymlíce,   þrísthycgende,
þæt þú þínne mǽgðhád   meotude brohtes,
sealdes bútan synnum.   Nán swylc ne cwóm
ǽnig óþer   ofer ealle men,
brýd béaghroden,   þe þá beorhtan lác
tó heofonháme   hlútre móde
siþþan sende.   Forðon héht sigores fruma
his héahbodan   hider gefléogan
of his mægenþrymme   ond þé meahta spéd
snúde cýðan,   þæt þú sunu dryhtnes
þurh clǽne gebyrd   cennan sceolde
monnum tó miltse,   ond þé, María, forð
efne unwemme   á gehealdan.
    Éac wé þæt gefrugnon,   þæt gefyrn bí þé
sóðfæst sægde   sum wóðbora
in ealddagum,   Ésaías,
þæt hé wǽre gelǽded   þæt hé lífes gesteald
in þám écan hám   eal scéawode.
Wlát þá swá wísfæst   wítga geond þéodland
oþþæt hé gestarode   þǽr gestaþelad wæs
æþelíc ingong.   Eal wæs gebunden
déoran since   duru ormǽte,
wundurclommum bewríþen.   Wénde swíðe
þæt ǽnig elda   ǽfre ne meahte
swá fæstlíce   forescyttelsas
on écnesse   ó inhebban,
oþþe ðæs ceasterhlides   clústor onlúcan,
ǽr him godes engel   þurh glædne geþonc
þá wísan onwráh   ond þæt word ácwæð:

"Ic þé mæg secgan þæt sóð gewearð
þæt ðás gyldnan gatu gíet sume síþe
god sylf wile gǽstes mægne
gefǽlsian, fæder ælmihtig,
ond þurh þá fæstan locu foldan néosan,
ond hío þonne æfter him éce stondað
simle singales swá beclýsed
þæt nǽnig óþer, nymðe nergend god,
hý ǽfre má eft onlúceð."
Nú þæt is gefylled þæt sé fróda þá
mid éagum þǽr on wlátade.
Þú eart þæt wealldor, þurh þé waldend fréa
ǽne on þas eorðan út síðade,
ond efne swá þec gemétte, meahtum gehrodene,
clǽne ond gecorene, Críst ælmihtig.
Swá ðé æfter him engla þéoden
eft unmǽle ǽlces þinges
lioþucǽgan biléac, lífes brytta.
Íowa ús nú þá áre þe sé engel þé,
godes spelboda, Gabriél brohte.
Húru þæs biddað burgsittende
þæt ðú þá frófre folcum cýðe,
þínre sylfre sunu. Siþþan wé mótan
ánmódlíce ealle hyhtan,
nú wé on þæt bearn foran bréostum stariað.
Geþinga ús nú þrístum wordum
þæt hé ús ne lǽte leng ówihte
in þisse déaðdene gedwolan hýran,
ac þæt hé úsic geferge in fæder ríce,
þær wé sorgléase siþþan mótan
wunigan in wuldre mid weoroda god.

X

Éalá þú hálga heofona dryhten,
þú mid fæder þínne gefyrn wǽre
efenwesende in þám æþelan hám.
Næs ǽnig þá gíet engel geworden,
ne þæs miclan mægenþrymmes nán
ðe in roderum up ríce biwitigað,
þéodnes þrýðgesteald ond his þegnunga,
þá þú ǽrest wǽre mid þone écan fréan
sylf settende þás sídan gesceaft,
bráde brytengrundas. Bǽm inc is gemǽne

héahgǽst hléofæst.   Wé þé, hǽlend Críst,
þurh éaðmédu   ealle biddað
þæt þú gehýre   hæfta stefne,
þínra níedþíowa,   nergende god,
hú wé sind geswencte   þurh úre sylfra gewill.
Habbað wræcmæcgas   wérgan gǽstas,
hetlen helsceaþa,   hearde genyrwad,
gebunden bealorápum.   Is séo bót gelong
eall æt þé ánum,   éce dryhten.
Hréowcearigum help,   þæt þín hidercyme
áfréfre féasceafte,   þéah wé fǽhþo wið þec
þurh firena lust   gefremed hæbben.
Ára nú onbehtum   ond usse yrmþa geþenc,
hú wé tealtrigað   týdran móde,
hwearfiað héanlíce.   Cym nú, hæleþa cyning,
ne lata tó lange.   Ús is lissa þearf,
þæt þú ús áhredde   ond ús hǽlogiefe
sóðfæst sylle,   þæt wé siþþan forð
þá sellan þing   symle móten
geþéon on þéode,   þínne willan.

XI

Éalá séo wlitige,   weorðmynda full,
héah ond hálig,   heofoncund þrynes,
bráde geblissad   geond brytenwongas
þá mid ryhte sculon   reordberende,
earme eorðware   ealle mægene
hergan héalíce,   nú ús hǽlend god
wǽrfæst onwráh   þæt wé hine witan móton.
Forþon hý, dǽdhwæte,   dóme geswíðde,
þæt sóðfæste   seraphinnes cynn,
uppe mid englum   á brémende,
unáþréotendum   þrymmum singað
ful héalíce   hlúdan stefne,
fægre feor ond néah.   Habbaþ folgoþa
cyst mid cyninge.   Him þæt Críst forgeaf,
þæt hý mótan his ætwiste   éagum brúcan
simle singales,   swegle gehyrste,
weorðian waldend   wíde ond síde,
ond mid hýra fiþrum   fréan ælmihtges
onsýne wréoð,   écan dryhtnes,
ond ymb þéodenstól   þringað georne
hwylc hyra néhst mæge   ussum nergende

flihte lácan   friðgeardum in.
Lofiað léoflícne   ond in léohte him
þá word cweþað,   ond wuldriað
æþelne ordfruman   ealra gesceafta:
"Hálig eart þú, hálig,   héahengla brego,
sóð sigores fréa,   simle þú bist hálig,
dryhtna dryhten!   Á þín dóm wunað
eorðlíc mid ældum   in ælce tíd
wíde geweorþad.   Þú eart weoroda god,
forþon þú gefyldest   foldan ond rodoras,
wígendra hléo,   wuldres þínes,
helm alwihta.   Síe þé in héannessum
éce hǽlo,   ond in eorþan lof,
beorht mid beornum.   Þú geblétsad léofa,
þe in dryhtnes noman   dugeþum cwóme
héanum to hróþre.   Þé in héahþum síe
á bútan ende   éce herenis."

XII

Éalá hwæt, þæt is wræclíc wrixl   in wera lífe,
þætte moncynnes   milde scyppend
onféng æt fǽmnan   flǽsc unwemme,
ond sío weres fríga   wiht ne cúþe,
ne þurh sǽd ne cwóm   sigores ágend
monnes ofer moldan;   ac þæt wæs má cræft
þonne hit eorðbúend   ealle cúþan
þurh gerýne,   hú hé, rodera þrim,
heofona héahfréa,   helpe gefremede
monna cynne   þurh his módor hrif.
Ond swá forðgongende   folca nergend
his forgifnesse   gumum tó helpe
dǽleð dógra gehwám,   dryhten weoroda.
Forþon wé hine dómhwate   dǽdum ond wordum
hergen holdlíce.   Þæt is héalíc rǽd
monna gehwylcum   þe gemynd hafað,
þæt hé symle oftost   ond inlocast
ond geornlícost   god weorþige.
Hé him þǽre lisse   léan forgildeð,
sé gehálgoda   hǽlend sylfa,
efne in þám éðle   þær hé ǽr ne cwóm,
in lifgendra   londes wynne,
þǽr hé gesǽlig   siþþan eardað,
ealne wídan feorh   wunað bútan ende. Ámén.